P9-DDN-280

There are a number of HORIZON CARAVEL BOOKS published each year. Titles now available are:

DESERT WAR IN NORTH AFRICA
THE BATTLE OF WATERLOO
THE HOLY LAND IN THE TIME OF JESUS
THE SPANISH ARMADA
BUILDING THE SUEZ CANAL
MOUNTAIN CONQUEST
PHARAOHS OF EGYPT
LEONARDO DA VINCI
THE FRENCH REVOLUTION
CORTES AND THE AZTEC CONQUEST
CAESAR
THE UNIVERSE OF GALILEO AND NEWTON
THE VIKINGS
MARCO POLO'S ADVENTURES IN CHINA
SHAKESPEARE'S ENGLAND
CAPTAIN COOK AND THE SOUTH PACIFIC
THE SEARCH FOR EARLY MAN
JOAN OF ARC
EXPLORATION OF AFRICA
NELSON AND THE AGE OF FIGHTING SAIL
ALEXANDER THE GREAT
RUSSIA UNDER THE CZARS
HEROES OF POLAR EXPLORATION
KNIGHTS OF THE CRUSADES

American Heritage also publishes AMERICAN HERITAGE JUNIOR LIBRARY books, a similar series on American history. Titles now available are:

THEODORE ROOSEVELT, THE STRENUOUS LIFE
GEORGE WASHINGTON AND THE MAKING OF A NATION
CAPTAINS OF INDUSTRY
CARRIER WAR IN THE PACIFIC
JAMESTOWN: FIRST ENGLISH COLONY
AMERICANS IN SPACE
ABRAHAM LINCOLN IN PEACE AND WAR
AIR WAR AGAINST HITLER'S GERMANY
IRONCLADS OF THE CIVIL WAR
THE ERIE CANAL
THE MANY WORLDS OF BENJAMIN FRANKLIN
COMMODORE PERRY IN JAPAN
THE BATTLE OF GETTYSBURG
ANDREW JACKSON, SOLDIER AND STATESMAN
ADVENTURES IN THE WILDERNESS
LEXINGTON, CONCORD AND BUNKER HILL
CLIPPER SHIPS AND CAPTAINS
D-DAY, THE INVASION OF EUROPE
WESTWARD ON THE OREGON TRAIL
THE FRENCH AND INDIAN WARS
GREAT DAYS OF THE CIRCUS
STEAMBOATS ON THE MISSISSIPPI
COWBOYS AND CATTLE COUNTRY
TEXAS AND THE WAR WITH MEXICO
THE PILGRIMS AND PLYMOUTH COLONY
THE CALIFORNIA GOLD RUSH
PIRATES OF THE SPANISH MAIN
TRAPPERS AND MOUNTAIN MEN
MEN OF SCIENCE AND INVENTION
NAVAL BATTLES AND HEROES
THOMAS JEFFERSON AND HIS WORLD
DISCOVERERS OF THE NEW WORLD
RAILROADS IN THE DAYS OF STEAM
INDIANS OF THE PLAINS
THE STORY OF YANKEE WHALING

A HORIZON CARAVEL BOOK

DESERT WAR
IN NORTH AFRICA

By the Editors of
HORIZON MAGAZINE

Author
STEPHEN W. SEARS

Consultant
MAJOR GENERAL I. S. O. PLAYFAIR C.B., D.S.O., M.C. (RET.)
British Military Historian for the Mediterranean and Middle East

Published by American Heritage Publishing Co., Inc.
Book Trade and Institutional Distribution by
Harper & Row

FIRST EDITION
Library of Congress Catalog Card Number: 67-20786

ULLSTEIN-BIRNBACK

Rommel, the Desert Fox, gets a battlefield report during the fighting at Tobruk in June, 1942, the time his generalship perhaps reached its peak.

FOREWORD

Great Britain's military fortunes were at a low ebb in January, 1942, as Prime Minister Winston Churchill stood before the House of Commons. "We have a very daring and skillful opponent against us," he remarked in a report on the fighting in North Africa, "and, may I say across the havoc of war, a great general." That so fierce and uncompromising a leader as Winston Churchill would publicly praise an enemy general, Germany's Erwin Rommel, is a measure of the unique character of the desert war.

The struggle for the North African coast of the Mediterranean—a struggle for oil and airfields and strategic position—was unlike any other campaign of World War II. This narrative of the three-year-long seesaw battle makes extensive use of eyewitness accounts and is illustrated with photographs, paintings, and drawings by men of the many nationalities who fought there.

The desert was an ideal testing ground for theories of warfare, particularly of armored warfare. Because it was fought like a tournament in an empty arena, with no one but the contestants getting hurt and with few of the distractions of politics or civilian populations, the desert war was a true test of generalship; commanders could weigh factors of manpower and weapons and supplies in planning tactics as if the desert were simply a huge chessboard. For these reasons, men like Germany's Rommel or Britain's Montgomery dominated the battle with the brilliance of their leadership as few other World War II generals were able to do. And for the same reasons, the desert war probably came closer to being fought within a set of reasonably civilized rules than any campaign of the twentieth century.

THE EDITORS

RIGHT: *Tankers of the British Eighth Army toast a desert victory atop the turret of their Matilda.*

COVER: *British Crusader tanks, photographed advancing across Egypt's Western Desert in 1942.*

FRONT ENDSHEET: *Hurricanes of the RAF patrol over Egypt in 1940. In foreground is the coast road.*

BACK ENDSHEET: *The Eighth Army takes a prisoner from a German tank at the El Alamein battle.*

ALL: IMPERIAL WAR MUSEUM, LONDON

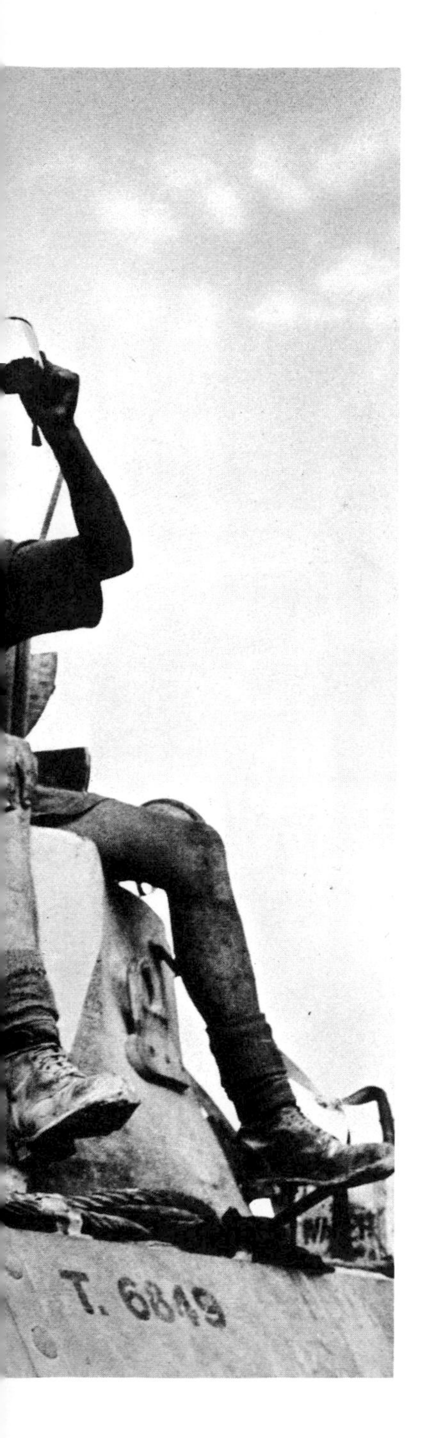

CONTENTS

I DESERT BATTLEGROUND

IMPERIAL WAR MUSEUM, LONDON

Marshal Rodolfo Graziani, governor general of the colony of Libya, commander in chief of the Italian Tenth Army, was most unhappy as he read his new orders. They came from Italy's head of state, the dictator Benito Mussolini, and they were blunt: attack within two days' time or face dismissal. Graziani was an impressive martial figure, full-fleshed and handsome, with silver hair and a noble profile, but he was far less confident than he looked. He believed that to attack now in the North African desert would be to court defeat; and defeat in the desert, he warned, would "inevitably develop into a rapid and total disaster."

As Marshal Graziani saw it on that September day in 1940, Italy was not prepared for war, certainly not war

British heavy artillery pounds the Italian defenses at Derna, a port in Libya, late in January of 1941. These guns, firing 55-pound shells some eleven miles, have camouflage nets to hide them from enemy planes.

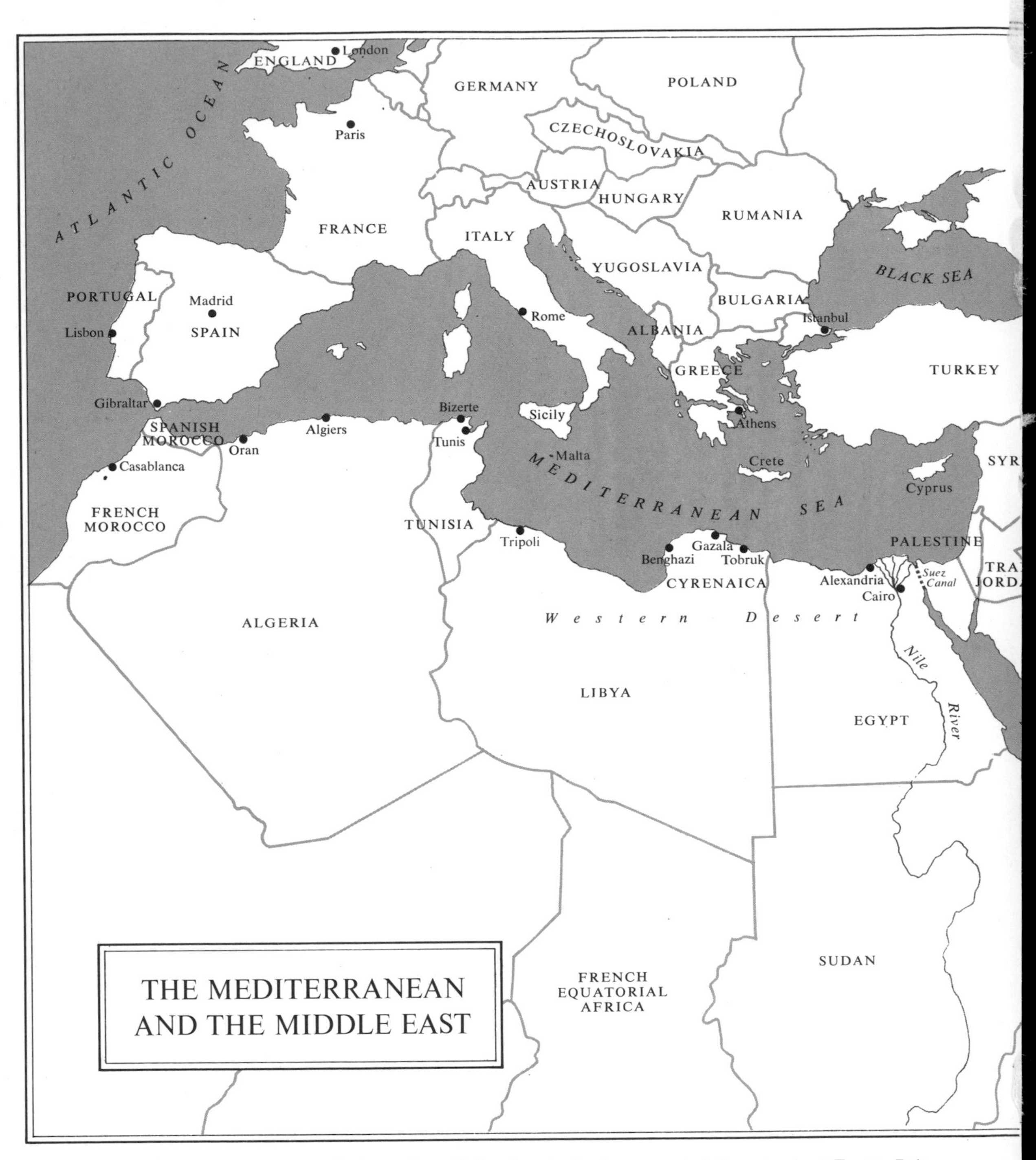

In September, 1940, when the Italian army in Libya struck at Egypt, British forces were stationed around the eastern rim of the Mediterranean to guard the Suez Canal (right center) and the oil fields of Iraq and the Persian Gulf area (far right). Britons and Italians also clashed in the countries of East Africa (lower right). French-held Tunisia, Algeria, and French Morocco (left) became neutral after Germany defeated France in June, 1940.

in North Africa. He knew what desert fighting was like. Before World War II he had led a campaign to conquer the Senussi, a tribe of Arabs rebelling against Italian rule in Libya, and the experience had been a sobering one. The desert was barren, featureless, and all but waterless. The difficulties of keeping an army supplied were staggering. Desert fighting imposed its own special rules, and Graziani suspected that his Tenth Army had not yet learned those rules.

All summer long he had been badgered to take the offensive. In June, 1940, Mussolini dragged Italy into World War II to pick up the spoils of victory and revive the glories of ancient Rome. Egypt, with her fertile Nile delta, her storied cities of Cairo and Alexandria, her famous Suez Canal, seemed to promise both. Push aside the small British army stationed there, said il Duce, and the prize will fall like a ripe plum; Graziani had 250,000 soldiers in Libya, surely enough for the job. By July Mussolini was writing Adolf Hitler, his fellow dictator in Germany, that "preparations for an attack on Egypt with vast objectives are now complete." As an observer remarked, "From a balcony in Rome, it looked easy."

Part of Graziani's reluctance to attack came from his cautious nature, part from shortages of such essentials of desert warfare as trucks, tanks, and antitank guns, and part from a healthy respect for his British opponents. While Mussolini harassed him from long distance, General Sir Archibald Wavell's Western Desert Force snapped at him from close range.

Hardly had Italy declared war before fast-moving British columns made up of tanks, armored cars, and artillery seized the Italian forts guarding the Egyptian-Libyan frontier. A few days later a well-armed Italian scouting force was ambushed and almost wiped out, losing seventeen tanks, a battery of field artillery, and some 100 men killed or captured; the British suffered no casualties at all. These hit-and-run raids continued through the summer. By September Graziani had lost 3,500 men, and Mussolini had lost his patience. From Rome came the curt order to attack.

On September 13, 1940, Graziani's Tenth Army heaved itself into motion at Sidi Omar, its advance base near the Egyptian frontier. For four days it rumbled eastward along the coast road paralleling the shore of the Mediterranean. Motorcyclists led the way, backed up by swarms of tanks and assault guns. Infantry followed in an endless procession of trucks. A small British rear guard fell back, persistently shelling the advancing Italians. At Sidi Barrani, a cluster of dusty, whitewashed mud huts 65 miles inside Egypt, Graziani halted and began building elaborate defenses. For the time being, at least, his offensive was over.

The Tenth Army came to a stop on September 16, and for nearly three months it made no further threatening moves. Graziani busied himself digging his army into a chain of fortified desert camps that stretched 50 miles south from Sidi Barrani. General Wavell put the three months to his own use, stockpiling supplies and laying his plans.

Archibald Wavell was square-jawed and solidly built, looking every inch the professional soldier. As a young officer he had served with the famous Black Watch in India, and during World War I he fought in France (where he lost an eye in combat) and in Palestine, in the Middle East. Between the wars his military education included service with Britain's newly formed armored force. His tanned, deeply lined face was usually expressionless, and his long silences were legendary throughout the British Army. But beneath this quiet mask was a man of great sensitivity and intelligence who wrote poetry to relax and who planned military operations with boldness and ingenuity. On August 2, 1939, he took command of the British Commonwealth forces in the Middle East. A month later Nazi Germany's assault on Poland triggered World War II.

Wavell's Middle East command included Egypt, the Sudan, East Africa, and the oil-rich lands around the Persian Gulf—nine countries in all, with a total area of almost three and a half million square miles. Some were British colonies; others, like Egypt, had signed treaties calling for protection by British forces. The Suez Canal was Britain's vital link to the Far East, but more important were the oil fields in Iraq and around the Persian Gulf upon which Britain's army, navy, and air force depended. Losing the Mediterranean and the Middle East would be a fatal blow to Great Britain's war effort.

There were many people in the United States and Europe who believed that Britain was doomed regardless of what happened in the Middle East. Her allies had collapsed one by one until she stood alone. In the spring of 1940 Hitler's blitzkrieg ("lightning war") engulfed Western Europe, defeating France and driving the British army on the Continent back across the English Channel. Grimly the British prepared for invasion while their fighter pilots battled the German Air Force in the skies above. As sum-

BLACK STAR

mer turned to fall, the invasion threat lessened, but now the Luftwaffe's planes poured bombs into London and other cities almost nightly. Britons at home read of Graziani's army camped within striking distance of the Suez Canal and complained bitterly about the do-nothings at "Headquarters Muddle East."

The fascist dictators, Germany's Hitler (left) and Italy's Mussolini, confer. In June of 1940, confident of an early end to the war, Mussolini wrote Graziani in North Africa: "I need a few thousand dead to justify my presence at the peace table."

Wavell's problems were many, large, and complex. His most pressing danger came from Graziani's 250,000 men at Sidi Barrani and in Libya, but there were another 350,000 Italian soldiers in East Africa for him to worry about. Wavell could count 86,000 troops throughout his entire Middle East command, most of them poorly equipped. He had kept Graziani at bay largely by a game of bluff. The trick, as a war correspondent described it, was to "make one man appear to be a dozen, make one tank look like a squadron, make a raid look like an advance." Finally, more tanks and guns and supplies arrived from England, and Wavell decided to stop bluffing and start fighting.

The Western Desert Force defending Egypt boasted two complete formations, the infantry of the 4th Indian Division and the Desert Rats of the 7th Armored Division, so called for the red jerboa, a small, ratlike desert creature, painted as an emblem on their vehicles. In command of the two divisions was Lieutenant General Richard O'Connor, a slight, shy, quiet-spoken man who, like Wavell, had in him a streak of boldness and a genius for command so highly prized in war.

In late October Wavell directed Western Desert Force headquarters to prepare a plan for an offensive against the Italians at Sidi Barrani. Ten days later O'Connor's plan was approved. Because Cairo, where Wavell had his headquarters, was so thick with spies that they all but stepped on one another's toes, only a handful of officers were told of the attack. O'Connor's army in the desert was sealed off by canceling all passes to Cairo and Alexandria. In the last week of November a training exercise was held. The troops attacked dummy "enemy camps" that exactly resembled those of the Italians, carefully photographed by planes of the Royal Air Force. O'Connor's offensive, code named Operation Compass, was to begin on December 7, 1940. On that day, to deceive enemy spies, Wavell appeared at the Cairo race track, and in the evening he was host to his top officers at a dinner party.

As Wavell played out his deception in Cairo, the army in the desert was stirring into action. "Just before dusk," wrote an officer of the 7th Armored Division, "we started the move forward. I can vividly remember watching the tanks ahead with their hulls hidden in drifting clouds of dust, but with each turret standing out clear and black against the fading western sky, each with two muffled heads emerging and two pennants fluttering above from the wireless aerial. Late at night we halted for refuelling and a few hours of sleep. . . . Daylight revealed a wonderful sight, the whole desert to the north covered with a mass of dispersed vehicles—tanks, trucks and guns all moving westwards with long plumes of dust rolling out behind. . . ."

ULLSTEIN-BIRNBACK

Marshal Rodolfo Graziani, head of Italy's army in North Africa, was photographed at Benghazi in 1940.

Through the day the advance continued. At noon an Italian reconnaissance plane was sighted, but it soared on unconcerned high overhead. That night the Western Desert Force leaped forward again until it lay within a few miles of Nibeiwa, one of the fortified Italian camps. A raid by RAF planes drowned out the noise of the truck engines and the clanking of tank tracks. By dawn on December 9 all units were in position. At a few minutes after 7 A.M. the British artillery opened up on Nibeiwa.

In terms of total manpower available to the two commanders, Graziani had an edge over O'Connor of ten to one. But in the vicinity of Sidi Barrani the Italians had only 120 tanks while their attackers had 275. More important, O'Connor had achieved complete surprise. He had penetrated a fifteen-mile gap between two Italian camps without being seen, putting his entire force right in the middle of the enemy position. (See map pages 20–21.)

The British shells falling into Nibeiwa had the same effect as a kick at an anthill. Soldiers rushed out of their tents in every direction. The crewmen of an armored battalion were warming up their tank engines and eating their breakfasts when the blow fell. In ten minutes most of them were casualties, and all 23 of their tanks were wrecked.

O'Connor's force barged into the camp, led by its heavy, slow-moving infantry tanks (called Matildas for their waddling, waltzing gait, like "Waltzing Matilda" in the song popular among the irrepressible Australian troops in the army). Trotting along behind the tanks came Indian infantrymen with fixed bayonets. The Italians fought back fiercely, but their bullets and hand grenades bounced harmlessly off the thick armored hide of the Matildas.

Within two hours the camp was in British hands. Some 2,000 prisoners were taken. The victors loaded themselves with fresh bread, vegetables, canned ham, and wine—Graziani's Italians were the best-provisioned army that fought in the desert war—and then pressed on northward

IMPERIAL WAR MUSEUM, LONDON

General Sir Archibald Wavell (right), commander in chief of the British forces in the Middle East, discusses the progress of Operation Compass with his field commander, General Richard O'Connor. They were photographed in the Western Desert in January, 1941.

through a sandstorm that covered the battlefield like a yellow fog. By nightfall Graziani's entire front was hopelessly shattered.

The next day the rest of the Italian camps were overrun or abandoned. Prisoners were taken faster than they could be counted. At Sidi Barrani a British officer radioed headquarters that his men were guarding "about five acres of officers and two hundred acres of other ranks." War correspondent Alan Moorehead reported standing on the coast road and watching prisoners march eastward on either side of the road in columns that stretched from horizon to horizon. By December 12, three days after the fighting began, the only Italians left in Egypt were in prisoner-of-war camps.

O'Connor pushed his men hard, using captured Italian trucks, gasoline, and food to keep rolling as the troops outran their own supply lines. When four of Graziani's divi-

IMPERIAL WAR MUSEUM, LONDON

Tobruk lies under a pall of smoke from supplies set ablaze by the Italian garrison before it surrendered. The two captured Italian tanks in the foreground are decorated with the kangaroo emblem of their Australian crewmen.

sions withdrew into the defenses of Bardia, a small port in Libya a few miles from the frontier, British armored forces swiftly reached around to cut the coast road behind them. Wavell sent up the 6th Australian Division to relieve the Indian infantry and lay siege to Bardia.

The Italian position was strong, with steel and concrete gun emplacements, thickly sown fields of explosive land mines, coils of barbed wire, and wide, steep-sided ditches to block tanks. On January 3, 1941, the Australians attacked. This time the infantry cleared the way for the tanks, reducing the strong points and filling in the antitank ditches. Then the Matildas moved in to complete the breach. Three Royal Navy battleships added a hail of 15-inch shells to the assault. The next day the tanks pushed on into Bardia itself. Still the Italians fought on, and not until January 5 was the last resistance overcome. In Bardia that night, correspondent Moorehead watched as "prisoners swarmed in every direction, and even in the light of the fires which were licking up the white walls of the houses it was impossible to distinguish enemy from friend. All they wanted was food, shelter from fighting, and a guarantee of life."

The spoils included 40,000 prisoners, 462 artillery pieces, 127 tanks, and more than 700 trucks. However, the garrison commander, General Annabale Bergonzoli, was nowhere to be found. Bergonzoli was called Electric Whiskers by his troops, who insisted that his bristling red beard gave off sparks. The Aussies resolved to catch Electric Whiskers and see this display for themselves.

Under O'Connor's prodding the Desert Rats of the 7th Armored Division thrust westward again and cut off the Italian garrison at Tobruk, 70 miles beyond Bardia. Once more the Australians came up to lay siege, and on January 21 they broke through the defenses. The next day Tobruk surrendered. A mountain of supplies was seized, and the bag of prisoners came to 25,000. Victorious Australians wandered through the town wearing swords and medals taken from Italian officers, gorging themselves on canned fruit, and lighting their cigarettes with Italian money. But Electric Whiskers again slipped through their fingers.

After Tobruk's fall Marshal Graziani gave up all hope of holding Cyrenaica, the northeastern part of Libya bulging out into the Mediterranean. As he had predicted, defeat had turned into disaster. His army proved to be as ponderous and slow moving as a dinosaur, unable to react to the swift slashes of its enemy. His tanks were outgunned and his generals outthought. Against O'Connor's driving leadership and well-trained desert fighters, the bravery of the individual Italian soldier went for nothing.

Graziani's Tenth Army retreated as fast as it could, mining the coast road behind it. Western Desert Force limped along in pursuit in a patchwork of battered vehicles, many of them captured and running on Italian gasoline. Both armies suffered alike from thirst and exhaustion.

At Mechili, a hundred miles west of Tobruk, O'Connor put everything into one final thrust to achieve total victory. The Desert Rats were down to 50 cruiser tanks (faster and lighter than the Matildas and intended for tank vs. tank fighting) and 95 light tanks armed only with machine guns. Their other vehicles were falling apart, and their supply situation was a shambles. Nevertheless, O'Connor sent the 7th Armored off on a short cut through the unmapped desert toward the coast road south of Benghazi to block the Italian retreat. The Australians would continue to pursue Electric Whiskers along the coast road and threaten Benghazi from the north.

On February 4 the Desert Rats and their bantam-sized Irish commander, Michael O'Moore Creagh, set off on the adventure. They immediately hit the worst going they had yet encountered in the desert, a 50-mile stretch of rock outcropping that chewed up tires and broke tank tracks. Soon the desert was littered with broken-down vehicles stripped of supplies and drained of gas and abandoned. When RAF reconnaissance planes reported that convoys of Italian trucks were beginning to head south from Benghazi, General Creagh assembled "Combeforce," a small, fast unit of trucks, guns, and armored cars under Lieutenant Colonel John Combe, to hurry ahead and block the coast road. Combeforce set out at top speed at dawn on February 5, and by noon it had reached the road near Beda Fomm. Within 30 minutes an Italian truck convoy from Benghazi ran into the ambush. O'Connor had won the race.

Meanwhile, Creagh's cruiser tanks were careering recklessly over the rough terrain at top speed to back up Combeforce with some firepower. At dusk they reached the road and immediately became embroiled with Italian tanks in a sharp battle fought by the light of burning vehicles.

Throughout the next day there was continuous, hard fighting in a driving rain. Vehicles by the hundreds piled up against the British roadblocks. Tanks and antitank guns dueled at point-blank range as the Italians desperately tried to break through. The few that did were picked

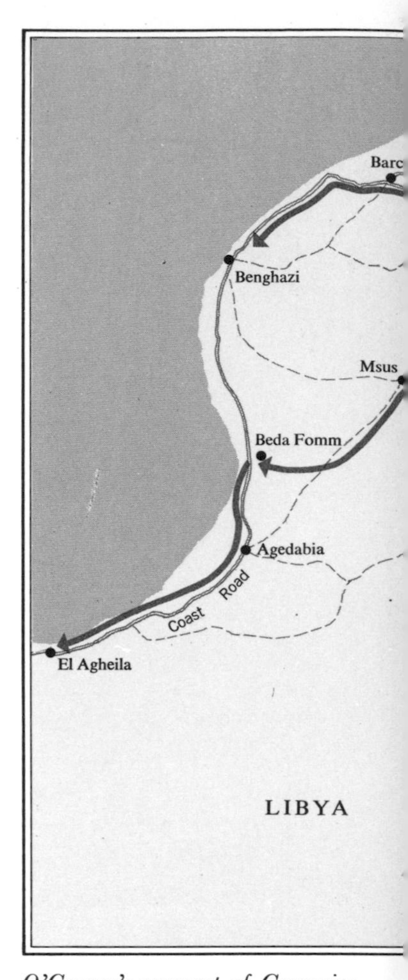

O'Connor's conquest of Cyrenaica is traced on the map above. The opening battle at Sidi Barrani is detailed in the inset; the 6th Australian Division replaced the 4th Indian infantry following this victory. At right is Italian general Annabale "Electric Whiskers" Bergonzoli. The picture was taken in 1937, when he commanded fascist troops in the Spanish Civil War.

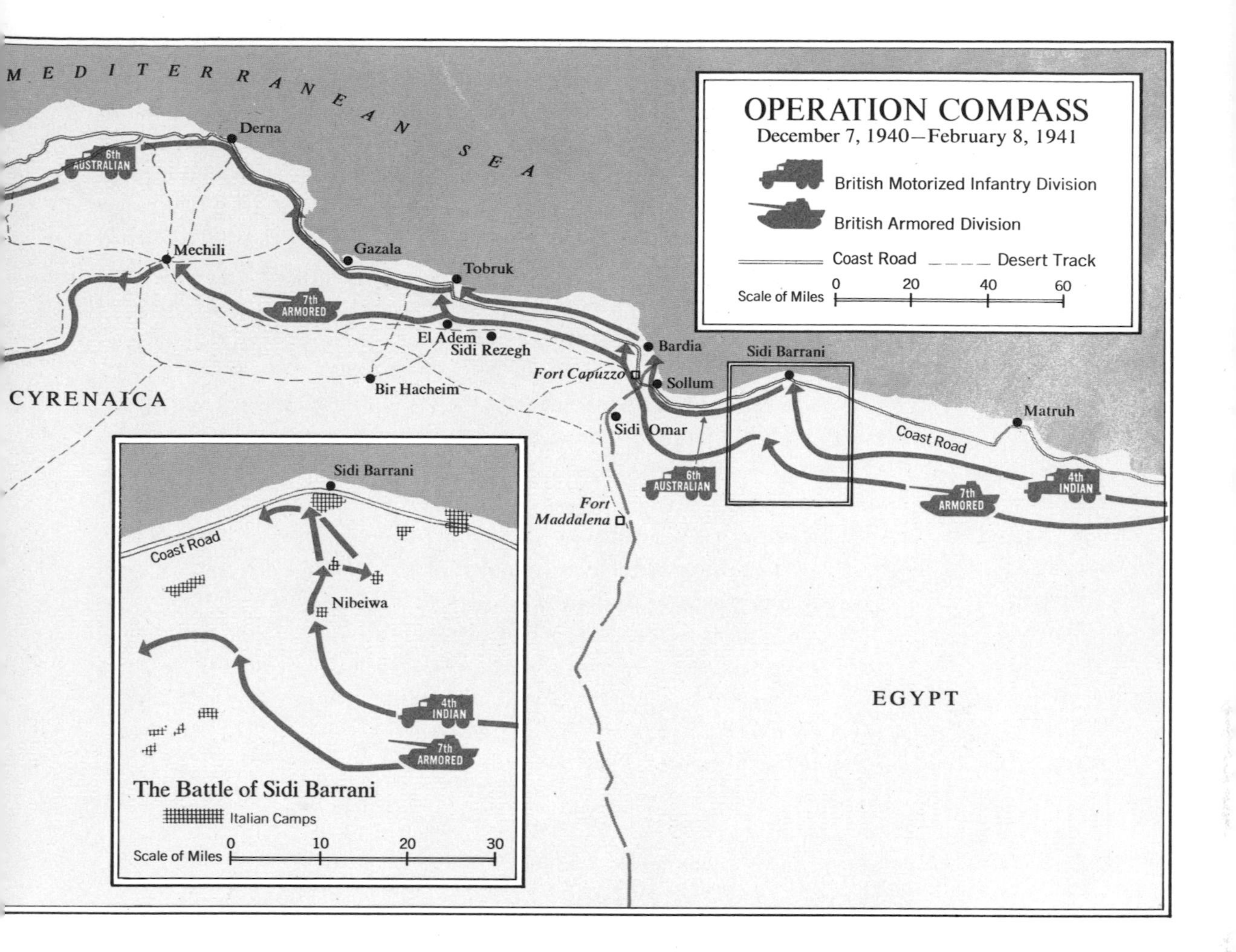

ULLSTEIN-BIRNBACK

off by Combeforce, lying in wait a few miles to the south.

The Battle of Beda Fomm was over on February 7, the same day that the Australians broke into Benghazi from the north. A war correspondent with the Desert Rats found the battlefield "strewn with broken and abandoned equipment, tattered uniforms, piles of empty shell and cartridge cases . . . littered with paper, rifles, and bedding. Here and there small groups of men tended the wounded who had been gathered together. Others were collecting and burying the dead. . . . Some equipment was still burning furiously."

Over 25,000 Italian soldiers and great stocks of equipment of every kind were captured at Beda Fomm and Benghazi. And this time Electric Whiskers did not escape. An armored car overtook him as he drove out of Benghazi. "You got here a bit too quickly today," Bergonzoli admitted sadly to his captors. Much to the disappointment of the Australians, he was hustled off to Cairo before they could test his famous beard.

In two months O'Connor had advanced 500 miles and conquered all of Cyrenaica. With a force never larger than 30,000 men, he had taken 130,000 prisoners, 380 tanks,

IMPERIAL WAR MUSEUM, LONDON

WIDE WORLD PHOTOS

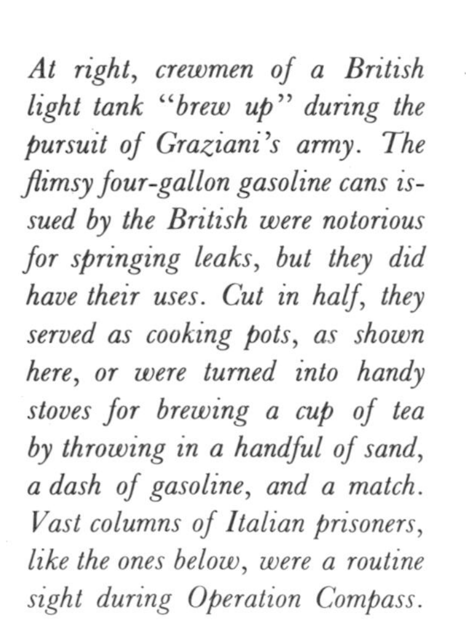

At right, crewmen of a British light tank "brew up" during the pursuit of Graziani's army. The flimsy four-gallon gasoline cans issued by the British were notorious for springing leaks, but they did have their uses. Cut in half, they served as cooking pots, as shown here, or were turned into handy stoves for brewing a cup of tea by throwing in a handful of sand, a dash of gasoline, and a match. Vast columns of Italian prisoners, like the ones below, were a routine sight during Operation Compass.

and almost 850 pieces of field artillery. His total casualties came to just over 1,900 killed, wounded, and captured. Operation Compass was one of the most startling triumphs of World War II, and the victory-starved British people greeted the news jubilantly.

O'Connor and Wavell immediately turned their thoughts to Tripoli, 500 miles to the west, Mussolini's last stronghold in North Africa. In London, however, the government of Prime Minister Winston Churchill had different plans. It decided it must honor a pledge to come to the aid of Greece, then teetering on the edge of war with Germany.

Western Desert Force was stripped to the bone to strengthen the Greeks. Wavell considered this an acceptable risk, for he believed Graziani's army was too badly mauled to do more than lick its wounds. He also had to keep up the pressure on the Italian army in East Africa. As soon as the campaigns in Greece and East Africa were over, he could rebuild the desert army and advance on Tripoli.

On February 12, 1941, five days after the Battle of Beda Fomm, Lieutenant General Erwin Rommel of the German Army stepped out of a plane at Tripoli. Adolf Hitler had decided to shore up his floundering Italian ally, and General Rommel was his choice to command the German units on their way to North Africa. Two days after his arrival, Rommel wrote his wife: "All going as well as I could wish. I hope to be able to pull it off. . . ."

II

ROMMEL TO THE RESCUE

Those who fought in the Western Desert, and those who reported the fighting there, devoted a good deal of effort to describing the setting. They noted the daytime heat and the nighttime cold, the swarming flies and the gritty, blowing sand, the spectacular sunsets and the star-filled night skies. And as they groped for a proper descriptive image, the one they most often hit upon was to compare the desert to the ocean.

More often than not, nothing but the unbroken line of the horizon could be seen in any direction. Vehicles moved freely across this waste like ships at sea. Men did not just drive in the desert, they navigated, getting where they wanted to go by using speedometer and map and compass. The few landmarks were usually man-made: a heap of rocks or empty gasoline cans, a stone cistern for catching rainwater, a whitewashed Moslem mosque, a long, lonely procession of telephone poles. The only paved road was the coast road. Inland, vehicles followed rough, dusty tracks that avoided the worst of the rocky outcroppings and the patches of soft sand.

From the shore of the Mediterranean, the Western Desert climbs upward in a haphazard series of steps, or escarpments. In most places these escarpments are too steep for trucks and even for tanks, and so the few natural gaps, or passes, in them became important military objectives. The surface of the desert is largely underlaid with limestone; tracked vehicles, at least, could drive almost anywhere on it. Only well inland does the true desert of drifting sand dunes begin. Narrow, stony ravines, called wadies, look from the air like jagged cracks. Here and there are large

Erwin Rommel (pointing) in his favorite spot—in the midst of battle. Rommel's habit of roaming the battlefield exasperated his staff, but he had the knack of being where he was most needed. Above: the Afrika Korps emblem.

ULLSTEIN-BIRNBACK

CAPTURED GERMAN PAINTING—U.S. ARMY

German artist Max Ohmayer painted one of Rommel's tanks in the Western Desert. It is the Panzer Mark IV type with a short-barreled 75-mm. gun.

dishlike depressions known as deirs. Inland from the sea, rain falls only two or three times a year, and in some places only once in two or three years.

A German general aptly described North Africa as a "tactician's paradise and a quartermaster's hell." The long, narrow desert battlefield stretched over 1,400 miles from Tripoli on the west, the Axis' major port, to Alexandria on the east, the Allies' chief base. The Germans and the Italians on the one hand and the British on the other were willing to spend their blood and treasure to win this desolate strip of land simply because neither side could afford to let the other have it. For the British the Western Desert was the buffer that protected the Suez Canal and the Middle Eastern oil fields, both of which the Axis powers wanted. In addition, whoever controlled the North African airfields was well ahead in the race to control the strategically vital Mediterranean.

BUNDESARCHIV, KOBLENZ

"Half the surface of the desert appeared to be in the air at one time," remarked a British officer of the sandstorms that plagued both armies. This German wears typical sandstorm gear—goggles and scarf.

As Marshal Graziani had ruefully noted, desert war imposed its own special rules. Rule number one was that armies brought with them everything they needed. There was no such thing as living off the country. As a result, the two most precious liquids were gasoline and water. For the British soldier, remarked a war correspondent, "The great problem in the mornings was to decide whether to make tea with the shaving water or to shave in the tea." What was left of a man's daily water ration (seldom more than a gallon) after drinking, cooking, bathing, and washing his clothes had to go into the radiator of his vehicle.

The second rule was the importance of total mobility. In the desert, infantrymen did not march; they rode in trucks. The queen of battle was the tank. Closely related to mobility was rule number three: the need for speed. A fast-moving, quick-off-the-mark army, as General O'Connor's Western Desert Force had proved, possessed an enormous edge; and a quick-thinking, energetic general could dominate an opponent who paused to gather up all the loose ends.

The final rule of desert warfare dealt with the nature of the battlefield itself. There were no industrial centers to capture, no captive populations to rule, no political considerations to clutter up tactics. It was a purely military struggle on an empty stage, and it was entirely possible to honor whatever "rules of the game" might still exist in a twentieth-century total war.

To meet the pressing needs in Greece and East Africa, General Wavell had left the Western Desert Force gravely weakened. "Next month or two will be anxious," he cabled Prime Minister Churchill in March, 1941, but he estimated that the enemy in Libya would not be strong enough to risk an attack before May. This, in fact, was precisely the timetable given in Hitler's orders to General Rommel. The turn of events was to surprise Hitler as much as Wavell.

Erwin Rommel was a forty-nine-year-old professional soldier whose reckless bravery during World War I had brought him two wounds and the Pour le mérite, Germany's highest military decoration. Outspoken and blunt, the son of a schoolteacher, Rommel lacked the arrogant polish of the Prussian aristocracy that supplied the German Army with so many of its officers. In the 1930's a book he wrote stressing boldness in infantry tactics caught Adolf Hitler's eye. In 1940, during the Battle of France, he led a panzer (armored) division with dash and brilliance. Hitler concluded that here was the man to pull Mussolini's chestnuts out of the fire. The moment Rommel set foot in North Africa, things began to happen.

Hitler had promised Mussolini an "Afrika Korps" of two German divisions, one armored and one of motorized infantry. When the 5th Light Motorized Division (a self-contained force of infantry, armor, artillery, and antitank and antiaircraft guns) arrived at Tripoli in February, 1941, Rommel ordered the ships unloaded right on through the night, ignoring the danger of an RAF bombing attack on the lighted docks. He put his engineers to building dummy wooden tanks atop little Volkswagen staff cars to make the British think he was stronger than he was. And he hurried his advance units to El Agheila, the westernmost British outpost in Libya, to test the enemy's strength.

The army that faced Rommel was not the fast-moving, quick-thinking force that had chased Marshal Graziani out of Egypt. The Desert Rats of the 7th Armored Division, back in Egypt for rest and refitting, had been replaced by the newly arrived 2nd Armored Division, green and at half strength. The 6th Australian Infantry, victors at Bardia and Tobruk and Benghazi, was relieved by another Australian division, untrained and poorly equipped. Replacing O'Connor in command was Lieutenant General Philip Neame, a newcomer to the desert.

On March 24, 1941, the German advance guard drove the British out of the El Agheila position. A week later Rommel launched a second probing attack. Sensing the weakness before him, he threw caution and orders to the wind. "It was a chance I could not resist," he wrote. By

IMPERIAL WAR MUSEUM, LONDON

A British scouting force, made up of a pair of light tanks and a supply truck, checks for signs of the enemy. In the background of this water color by war artist A. A. Gregson is a clifflike desert escarpment.

April 2 Neame's defenses were splintered, and orders went out to abandon Benghazi if necessary. Wavell ordered General O'Connor to fly at once to Cyrenaica to try to restore a defensive front.

There was little O'Connor could do, for Western Desert Force was rapidly falling apart. Communications broke down, orders were bungled, troops went astray. An enormous supply dump containing most of the 2nd Armored's gasoline was set afire by its guards when they thought the enemy was approaching; the "enemy" turned out to be a British patrol.

As O'Connor had done earlier in the year, Rommel took the desert short cut across the base of the Cyrenaican "bulge." He pushed his men relentlessly, flying from one column to another in his tiny Storch observation plane. When told that the vehicles needed servicing and repairs, he ordered his officers not to bother with such "trifles." The 5th Light Division's commander asked for a four-day halt to bring up ammunition and gasoline; Rommel had him empty all his trucks—leaving the division stranded immobile in the desert for 24 hours—and send them back to depots to bring up the needed supplies. An Italian general complained that he was being ordered into impassable terrain; Rommel drove ahead a dozen miles by himself to prove the route was clear.

Late on the night of April 3, Rommel paused long enough to write his wife. "We've been attacking since the 31st with dazzling success," he told her. "There'll be consternation amongst our masters in Tripoli and Rome, and perhaps in Berlin too. I took the risk against all orders and instructions because the opportunity seemed favorable. . . . You will understand that I can't sleep for happiness." By April 6 most of the Cyrenaican bulge was in Axis hands. Benghazi had fallen, and the spread fingers of Rommel's probing columns were reaching for Mechili, where the exhausted British were regrouping.

That night a British staff car drove headlong into a German scouting force on one of the desert tracks north of Mechili. There was a brief exchange of gunfire in the darkness, killing the British driver and a German motorcyclist. The staff car was surrounded, and the occupants were ordered to surrender. Out stepped generals Neame and O'Connor and Brigadier John Combe, whose Combeforce had slammed the door on the retreating Italians barely two months before. (So seriously did Wavell feel O'Connor's loss that he tried—unsuccessfully—to exchange him

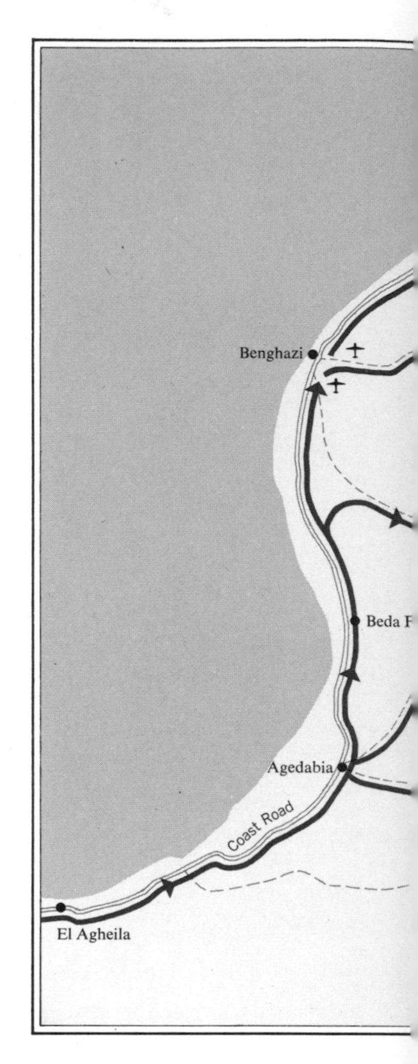

BUNDESARCHIV, KOBLENZ

German machine gunners and a radioman at the siege of Tobruk.

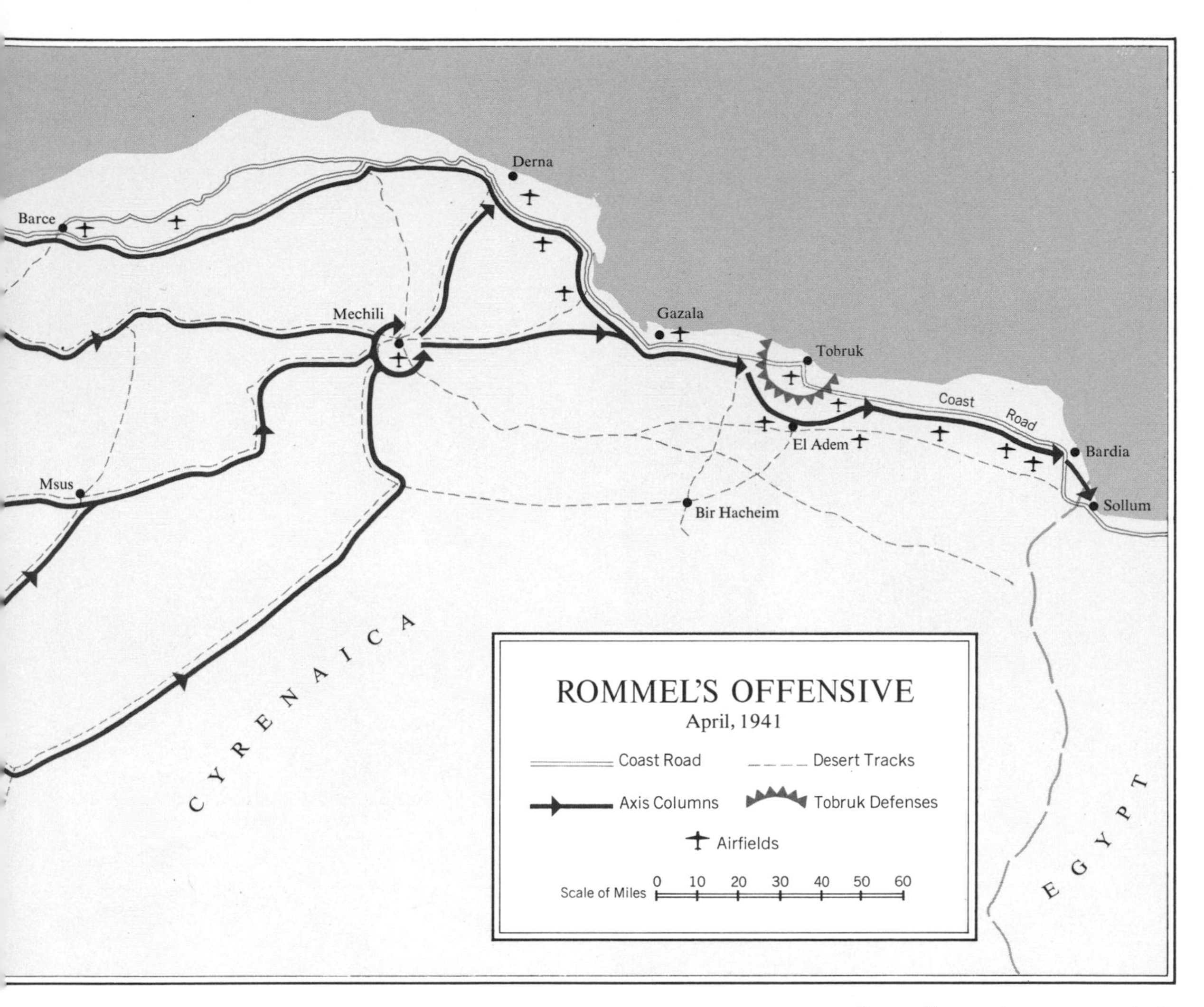

Rommel's surprise counterstroke in April of 1941 retook all of Cyrenaica, lost by Marshal Graziani's Italian army, except for Tobruk.

for any six captured Italian generals that Mussolini's high command cared to choose.)

The next day Mechili fell. The British streamed on eastward. Most of the Australian infantry reached safety in the defenses of Tobruk, but the 2nd Armored Division was shattered; it never again appeared on the battle roles of the British Army. Seeking a quick victory, Rommel hurled his troops at Tobruk. But his planning was too hurried and his men too exhausted, and the assault was beaten off. German armored forces bypassed the fortress and seized Bardia and Sollum, key points along the coastal escarpment. Cyrenaica had been regained, and once more the Axis were at the gates of Egypt.

April, 1941, was a month of severe trial for Great Britain. Only the campaign against the Italians in East Africa

went well. Officials in London sugar-coated the defeat in the Western Desert with such phrases as "a withdrawal to a battleground of our own choosing" and "part of a plan for an elastic defence," but few Britons were fooled. On April 6 Hitler attacked Yugoslavia, whose capital, Belgrade, fell within a week. Greece too was invaded. The forces sent there at such cost by Wavell could not stem the Nazi tide, and by the end of the month they had to be evacuated. The British island of Malta, key to control of the Mediterranean, was savagely pounded by the Luftwaffe. Oil-rich Iraq, east of Suez, was torn by an anti-British revolt, and there were signs that a similar revolt was brewing in Syria. In a grim mood, Churchill wrote President Franklin D. Roosevelt: "In this war every post is a winning-post, and how many more are we going to lose?"

As usual, Churchill met trouble head on by bounding into action. Axis submarines, warships, and planes were so thick in the Mediterranean that British ships carrying supplies to the Middle East took the slow, 14,000-mile route around Africa and through the Red Sea to Egypt. Now, overriding the objections of his military advisers, Churchill ordered the Royal Navy to force a passage through the Mediterranean with a convoy of merchant ships carrying tanks to General Wavell. The code name for his bold plan was Operation Tiger.

It would have comforted the Prime Minister to know that just then all was not serene in the Axis camp. Rommel was determined to press on into Egypt and beyond as soon as he was re-supplied and the Tobruk thorn was removed from his flank. But his unexpected victories had embarrassed the Nazi high command. It had not intended North Africa to be a major theater of war. General Franz Halder, chief of the German General Staff, complained grumpily in his diary that Rommel did not even submit proper reports; instead, "All day long he rushes about between his widely scattered units." Something must be done to "head off this soldier gone stark mad," Halder thought, or he would embroil Germany in a campaign beyond her resources.

Shrugging off his first repulse at Tobruk, Rommel searched for a weak spot in its defenses. Tobruk was im-

A dogfight over Malta, by British artist Denis Barnham. The view is from the cockpit of an RAF Spitfire (a second Spitfire is visible in its rear-view mirror) locked in a duel with a German Messerschmitt 109. In the background is a formation of twin-engined German Junkers 88 bombers.

INCIDENT AT TOBRUK

During the eighth-month siege of Tobruk in 1941, the garrison averaged 23,000 fighting men, some 15,000 of them Australians. Their only link to the outside world was by sea. The RAF had to withdraw its fighters from Tobruk in the face of heavy Axis air attacks, leaving it unprotected, and hardly a day went by when there was not at least one raid. This is how one such raid, by German dive bombers, looked to an infantry platoon of the 9th Australian Division. It is from Eric Lambert's novel The Twenty Thousand Thieves*; although it is fiction, it has the authentic ring of an eyewitness report.*

It was an ordinary Libyan day, furnace-hot with a glare that was like a knife across the eyes. Striking the stone-littered surface of the desert the light quivered vaporously. The sky was the color of smoke. It was motionless. The sun was seen through it like a coin in a dim pool.

But there was life in that sky.

Six Platoon sat in their pits. They were not the men who, attired correctly and uniformly, had marched around the roads of Palestine or stalked the streets of Jerusalem and Tel Aviv in quest of adventures. Their shorts were bleached to a dirty yellow and their boots were worn to whiteness by the sand. Gone was the slouch hat; in its place they wore the round steel helmet, painted yellow. Those who had discarded their shirts showed skins as brown as the wood in the butts of their rifles. Their eyes were keener, their faces leaner, their lips drawn finer. . . .

The whole platoon busied itself in a casual sort of fashion. Then, with one accord, they stopped and looked upwards. There was a faint pulsing in the sky. . . . The pulsing became a trembling, the trembling became a hum. Then suddenly the noise of the dive bombers burst out of the blue like a snarl.

"Here they are," cried Dick, and pointed to the east.

They came out of the sun, black and evil-looking Stukas. Their curiously shaped wings were like those of hawks, poised to drop on their prey. There were two flights of them. One flight peeled off, dwindling in the direction of the invisible town.

The world became all noise. Around them the Bofors guns coughed out a torrent of explosions and the sky flowered with little white pom-poms of smoke. Farther back the heavy anti-aircraft brayed hideously upwards.

One by one the black shapes came earthwards, as if they hurtled down a gigantic slide. The shrieks of their downward passage pierced the sound of exploding bombs. The earth around the Australians vomited upwards in great black clouds.

The air became a fog of yellow dust and black smoke and through the frightful din came faintly the cries of men. . . .

Then, as suddenly as it began, the raid ceased. The anti-aircraft fire dwindled to isolated bangs. The noise of the Stukas grew fainter and fainter in the distance. Human voices carried through the drifting smoke. One of the voices called, high-pitched and urgent: "Stretcher-bearer!" Forms came running through the haze. . . .

Six Platoon came out of their pits to discover who were their latest casualties. Dick clambered across the parapet and made towards the wadi where men were already gathered. . . .

The two dead men had been placed on stretchers. Neither of them was well-known to Dick. One was a small grey man approaching middle age who had joined the battalion only a few days before it left Palestine. His remains formed an unnatural heap beneath a blanket through which the blood oozed. The other lay uncovered, his eyes looking sightlessly to the sky. None of Six Platoon had known him very well either. He had been a big, fair, smiling young fellow, always pleasant, but shy. All they knew about him was that he had been a motor mechanic and had a young wife to whom he wrote every day. He was not marked, but his clothes hung from him in a thousand small tatters where the blast had ripped across his body.

Watched by the men of Six Platoon, the stretcher-bearers bore the dead men slowly down the wadi. Andy gazed expressionlessly after them.

"That's that," he said.

ULLSTEIN-BIRNBACK

This German photograph shows a Stuka dive bomber pulling away after blasting the defenders of Tobruk. The British lost 34 warships and merchant ships, most of them to air attacks, in supplying their besieged garrison.

portant to him because of its harbor, the only one of any size between Alexandria and Benghazi. The desert around the small, whitewashed town was flat as a plate; the verdict of one observer was that it "must have been difficult to defend even in the days of bows and arrows." Yet before the war the Italians had lavished many tons of concrete and steel on its defenses.

A double row of strong points and trenches formed a semicircle 30 miles in length around the harbor. The British strengthened this line with barbed wire, tank traps, mine fields, and a heavy concentration of artillery. The garrison, made up mostly of Australian infantry supported by a few tanks, was led by General Leslie Morshead. He and his Aussies were very tough and very determined. "There is to be no surrender and no retreat," Morshead told his officers.

Rommel hurled three major assaults against the Australians, using a variety of tactics. But his forces were too weak, and the opposition too determined, to achieve a breakthrough. By May he had to content himself with tightening the ring around the fortress while he waited impatiently for the reinforcements he needed to attack again.

The siege of Tobruk was to drag on for eight months, until the winter of 1941. It was a boring, bloody, dangerous stalemate for the men on both sides. They "went to ground" during the day, suffering the stifling heat and the swarming insects to avoid sniper's bullets. Bombing and artillery fire took a steady toll. The desolate landscape, wrote a British war correspondent, was "littered with broken transport, burned-out tanks, and spent ammunition, as though some junk merchant had set up business on the surface of the moon." Morshead's garrison could be supplied only by ship, and only at night, and British naval losses were heavy. But neither side would loosen its grip. To the British Commonwealth, Tobruk came to stand for stubborn courage in the face of adversity. To Rommel, Tobruk was a symbol of frustration. He vowed that someday the fortress would be his.

BOTH: IMPERIAL WAR MUSEUM, LONDON

General Leslie Morshead, commander of the Tobruk garrison, shown outside his headquarters.

For General Wavell, events in his command were fast reaching a climax. Coolly he moved his available forces across the vast chessboard of the Middle East—to put down revolts in Iraq and Syria, to gain final victory over the Italians in East Africa, to probe Rommel's outposts on the Egyptian frontier, to counter (unsuccessfully) a massive assault on the island of Crete by Nazi paratroopers. All the while a blizzard of telegrams from Churchill, all crying for action, descended on Wavell's Cairo headquarters.

On May 12, 1941, the Tiger convoy anchored at Alexandria, having lost only one ship in the Mediterranean passage and bringing Wavell 238 tanks. Churchill, who had risked so much to get this reinforcement to the Middle East, waited anxiously for his Tiger Cubs, as he called them, to go into action. Wavell replied that Operation Battleaxe was scheduled for June 15. He intended to use the new tanks to break Rommel's shield at Sollum and Bardia, then advance 70 miles westward to lift the siege of Tobruk. The Desert Rats of the 7th Armored Division would make up the spearhead of the attack.

Battleaxe called for the 4th Indian Division, supported by infantry tanks, to capture Halfaya Pass, an important gap in the coastal escarpment near Sollum. The British armor would meanwhile swing around to the left beyond the Axis positions guarding Sollum and Bardia. Here, on the desert flank, Wavell saw the decisive tank battle taking place.

On the appointed morning eighteen Matildas waddled toward Halfaya Pass, followed by Indian infantrymen in

Capturing the captors: British infantrymen seize a German tank crew that was manning a captured British Matilda, which the tankers had prudently marked with Nazi insignia so they would not be shot at by their comrades. The Germans admired the heavily armored Matilda and made use of any they took.

trucks. Before the tanks were close enough to fire effectively with their own guns, they were hit by a hail of armor-piercing shells. Eleven of the twelve leading Matildas stopped dead, some in flames, others with gun turrets blown completely off their hulls. Four others behind them withdrew, blundered into a mine field, and had tracks blown off. Later the same day, far out on the desert flank, a column of British cruiser tanks met the same kind of devastating fire from a German strong point.

Thus were British armored forces introduced to the German 88-millimeter gun, one of the best artillery pieces of World War II. A dual-purpose antiaircraft and antitank gun, the long-barreled 88 was accurate and fast firing, and its 21-pound shell had tremendous hitting power; at a range of well over a mile it could kill even the most heavily armored tank with a single shot. Rommel had only a dozen of these guns, but the five at Halfaya Pass, for example, had been dug into stony clefts so that the barrels were at ground level. In the shimmering desert haze and with their flashless charges they were all but invisible.

On the second day of Battleaxe, Rommel threw in the tanks of the 5th Light Division and the newly arrived 15th

Panzer Division, the second of the two divisions Hitler had promised Mussolini. While neither side could claim a clear-cut advantage, Rommel was beginning to gain the upper hand. Most of his outposts, including Halfaya Pass (by now, and ever after, known to the British as Hellfire Pass), had held firm. The 5th Light was on the flank of the Desert Rats, and the German armor was better concentrated. Most important, Rommel had taken the measure of the British field commanders and found them cautious and unimaginative, and he was ready to seize the initiative. He would "deal the enemy an unexpected blow in his most sensitive spot" by a flank attack at first light on June 17, before the British could launch any attack of their own.

From here on Rommel stayed a step ahead of his enemy. By four in the afternoon of June 17 his panzer columns were hooking in toward Halfaya Pass, and the British were rushing eastward to escape encirclement. The British lost 27 cruiser tanks and 64 Matildas—almost half their armored force. The Afrika Korps won the battlefield as well as the battle and recovered and repaired its damaged tanks; in all, Rommel had but a dozen tanks destroyed.

From the failure of Battleaxe the British concluded that their tanks were outgunned by those of the enemy, which was not true. This error grew out of the larger misunderstanding about what had killed so many of their cruisers and Matildas. They believed German tanks were responsible, when in most cases the actual killers were antitank guns, particularly the 88. The failure to appreciate the full value of antitank guns, or how Rommel was using them, was to haunt the British in the months to come.

When the Battleaxe reports reached England, Winston Churchill was at Chartwell, his country home, where he had gone to await the outcome. There he received news of the defeat. "A most bitter blow," he wrote, "I wandered about the valley disconsolately for some hours." Beyond the fact that his beloved Tiger Cubs had been so roughly handled was the grimmer realization that for the first time the desert army had struck a full-strength blow, only to be repulsed.

The Middle East needed new blood, Churchill believed. He had lost confidence in General Wavell. On June 21 he cabled Wavell that "the victories which are associated with your name will be famous in the story of the British Army," but that "the public interest will best be served" by a change in command. The new Commander in Chief Middle East was to be General Sir Claude Auchinleck. Wavell

Afrika Korps gunners manhandle a trailer-mounted 88-mm. antitank gun into position. No other weapon in the desert war was more feared than the 88; the white rings around the barrel of the one pictured here indicate that its crew claimed the destruction of eight British tanks.

would take Auchinleck's place as head of British Commonwealth forces in India.

Wavell received the news from an aide early the next morning in his Cairo home. He was shaving. He showed no emotion as he listened to the orders, remarked quietly that "the Prime Minister's quite right—this job needs a new eye and a new hand," and went on shaving. He took his usual morning ride and swim and then set about getting things in order for his successor.

For nearly two years, in victory and defeat, Archibald Wavell had kept the Middle East in the Allied column. Certainly no other British soldier in World War II shouldered so many burdens. He built the foundations for victories that other men would win. When the change of command was made public, correspondent Alan Moorehead wrote: "There went out of Cairo and the Middle East that afternoon one of the great men of the war."

ULLSTEIN-BIRNBACK

III STRIKE

AND COUNTERSTRIKE

IMPERIAL WAR MUSEUM, LONDON

On June 22, 1941—the same day that General Wavell learned he was no longer Commander in Chief, Middle East—the war in Europe took a startling new turn. With a mass of men and machines totaling 120 divisions, Adolf Hitler launched Operation Barbarossa, a surprise attack on Russia. To North Africa went Hitler's orders to "march in place" for the three or four months he predicted it would take to destroy the Russian Red Army.

Axis strategists foresaw glittering opportunities in Barbarossa. The conquest of southern Russia, they calculated, would become the upper jaw of an enormous pincers movement overwhelming the Middle East. Properly reinforced, Rommel would then sweep aside the British, thrust through Egypt, Palestine, Syria, and Iraq, force neutral Turkey to terms, and close the pincers in Persia. The Mediterranean would become an Axis lake; the Middle Eastern oil fields would fill the Nazi war machine to capacity; the British would be severed from their empire and helpless.

No one saw this bright promise more clearly than Erwin Rommel, yet he knew that for him the next few months would be crucial. He could expect no substantial reinforcements to be diverted from the Russian front. "It's all quiet here so far," he wrote his wife early in July. "But I'm not being taken in. Our stubborn friends on the other side will be back sooner or later."

Rommel's "stubborn friends" did indeed plan to test him again. Through the summer and fall of 1941 General Auchinleck rebuilt, reorganized, and even renamed his army. The desert force became the Eighth Army, under the field command of General Sir Alan Cunningham. Planes, tanks, guns, trucks, and men by the thousands poured into

An American-built Curtiss Kittyhawk fighter-bomber, painted to resemble a shark, was sketched by war artist Anthony Gross at an RAF desert airfield.

IMPERIAL WAR MUSEUM, LONDON

The piratical-looking men at left, who belonged to the British Special Air Service (SAS), attacked supply depots and airfields deep behind Axis lines. They mounted machine guns on jeeps and carried extra gasoline in captured German fuel cans. At right, a pair of German armored cars engage in a night battle near Tobruk in November, 1941.

Egypt from Great Britain; planes and tanks also came from American factories under the Lend-Lease program.

As the curve of British strength climbed upward, Rommel's strength did not keep pace. Shortages of all kinds appeared as the RAF and the Royal Navy slashed at his vulnerable supply line across the Mediterranean. In September, 1941, 28 per cent of all Axis cargoes were lost, and in November the figure leaped to 63 per cent. In a night attack that month a force of British warships pounced on a seven-ship convoy bound for Tripoli and sent all seven, plus an escorting Italian destroyer, to the bottom.

While the opponents gathered their forces for the battle both knew was coming, the siege of Tobruk dragged on, and skirmishes flickered around the outposts of the two armies. As patrols probed for information, the humped silhouettes of British armored cars and the squat, angular shapes of German cars became familiar sights on the horizon. Often they clashed, racing at each other in quick, darting sallies, blazing away with machine guns, skidding and swerving and throwing up plumes of dust. The loser might be left canted over crazily in the sand under a spiral of oily

ULLSTEIN-BIRNBACK

black smoke, like some vanquished mechanical gladiator.

The search for accurate intelligence about enemy positions and movements never ceased. Armored-car patrols was one method. Another was aerial reconnaissance, an especially effective way to gain information quickly during a battle. A third way was to send parties of daring men deep behind enemy lines.

German units known as Brandenburgers penetrated into the rear of the Eighth Army, sometimes nearly to Cairo, to gather information and attack supply lines. A better-known—and more successful—British unit called the Long Range Desert Group sent small parties of men in light trucks around the desert flank and well behind the enemy. Lurking near ports and along the coast road and the main desert tracks, these parties radioed back information about the arrival of supply ships and kept track of the reinforcements sent forward to the Axis fighting forces. In November, 1941, a special group tried to kill or capture Rommel by raiding his headquarters. But he was not there, and most of the raiders were killed or captured themselves.

Another British unit, the Special Air Service (a cover

name to keep its real activities secret), not only gathered intelligence but spread havoc wherever it went. Set up in the summer of 1941 after Operation Battleaxe, the SAS's guiding genius was a handsome, six-foot-six, black-bearded young officer named David Stirling, the Phantom Major.

Ranging as far as 350 miles behind enemy lines, and staying there weeks at a time, SAS men became a serious menace to Rommel's supply lines and air support. They buried mines in the coast road, blew up gasoline stocks and supply dumps, attacked truck convoys, and shot up parked planes on airfields. In fourteen months of action, before Stirling himself was captured, the SAS claimed the destruction of 250 German and Italian planes.

A typical display of SAS daring was a raid that Stirling and two companions made on a German airfield near Benghazi. Approaching the field on a moonless night, they found two parked Messerschmitt 110 fighters. After attaching incendiary bombs with one-hour fuzes to the planes,

Edward Copnall painted an Eighth Army unit preparing its Valentine infantry-support tanks for action. The tent at right gave shelter to mechanics fixing the tank's engine. Tank "leaguers," or encampments, were widely separated to make air attacks less effective.

they turned to the hangars and workshops. They slipped into the first hangar, found it filled with machinery and tools, and planted more bombs. In the next hangar four mechanics were repairing an engine. Keeping in the shadows, Stirling quietly placed a bomb in a Junkers transport plane only a few feet from the Germans. In the third hangar the raiders found two more Junkers and stacks of crated aircraft engines, some 40 in all. While one kept watch for patrolling guards, the other two planted bombs. It took them twenty minutes; now they were setting fuzes for less than half an hour.

After coming within a hairbreadth of bumping into guards in the darkness, Stirling decided to cap the night's work with a direct attack. As the time neared for the bombs to explode, he kicked open the door of the crowded guardroom and threw in a hand grenade. "We then ran like hell," one of his men wrote. "The bombs in the hangars had also started to go off. As we got clear we stopped to

IMPERIAL WAR MUSEUM, LONDON

look. One of the 110's on the field went up, and cannon started to explode with the heat. It was a pretty picture as the JU's in the hangars began to burn."

To spearhead the offensive (Operation Crusader) he had scheduled for November, General Cunningham put nearly all his armor—4th, 7th, and 22nd armored brigades, averaging 155 cruiser tanks each—into the 30th Corps under General Willoughby Norrie. He massed his infantry in another corps, the 13th, under General A. R. Godwin-Austen, and stiffened it with a brigade of 135 infantry tanks. Cunningham, whose brother commanded the Royal Navy in the Mediterranean, had made his mark beating the Italian army in East Africa, where he collected over 200,000 prisoners. This was to be his first chance to command a "tank army."

UPI

Alan Cunningham, Eighth Army commander in Operation Crusader.

On the fighting line, then, the Eighth Army could count some 600 tanks, with 100 more in besieged Tobruk and 200 in reserve. Cunningham intended to swing the armor of the 30th Corps around the desert flank of Rommel's frontier positions at Sollum and Bardia, drawing the German general into a great tank battle. Once the panzer divisions were broken, the infantry of the 13th Corps would move in, mop up, and lift the siege of Tobruk. As to how the battle itself would be fought, Cunningham said, "My plans depend very much on what old Rommel decides to do."

Although the Axis forces received no important reinforcements after Operation Battleaxe, some changes had been made. Rommel's major striking force remained the Afrika Korps, reorganized into three divisions—the 15th Panzer, the 21st Panzer (the old 5th Light Division renamed), and the 90th Light, an infantry division assembled from miscellaneous units—all under the command of General Ludwig Cruwell. The bulk of Rommel's manpower was still Italian infantry.

The Eighth Army had a superiority in tanks of about 700 to Rommel's 390. Nearly half of General Norrie's cruiser tanks were the new Crusaders, from which the offensive took its name. They were fast and well armored, but they were proving distressingly weak mechanically. The Crusader, like the Matilda and its replacement, the Valentine, was armed with a 2-pounder gun (named for the weight of its shell, 40-mm. in diameter). From America had come the Stuart, mechanically sound and at 40 miles an hour the fastest tank in the desert. Its high-velocity 37-mm. gun hit slightly harder than the 2-pounder, but its aircraft-type engine used so much gasoline that its combat

Water cans are unloaded at a forward supply dump in this painting by German artist Helmut Georg. The camouflage netting shown here was effective in concealing supplies from aerial reconnaissance.

range was short. The Stuart was popular with British tank crews, who christened it the Honey (a tanker described it as "a honey" after a test drive, and the name stuck).

On the Axis side the work-horse tank was the Panzer Mark III, reliable, built low to the ground, and mounting a short-barreled 50-mm. gun with about the same hitting power as the 2-pounder; its armor was somewhat thin, however. Rommel also had 35 of the Panzer Mark IV type. Its stubby 75-mm. gun was best suited to firing high-explosive shells at enemy infantry and artillery positions. His 70 Mark II light tanks mounted only heavy machine guns, and his 146 Italian tanks had poor armor and were liable to break down at any time.

The Afrika Korps did have an edge over the Eighth

A British column creates a fog of dust as it advances across the desert during the Crusader offensive. "Tanks and supply columns maneuvered there like great squadrons of vessels at sea," wrote correspondent Alan Moorehead of this battle.

Army in the quality of its antitank guns. The 88-mm. was in a class by itself, although in the fall of 1941, Rommel had only 35 of them. He had almost a hundred of the handy 50-mm. antitank guns, which outhit and outranged the 2-pounder the British used as both a tank and antitank gun.

There were other, more basic, differences in the two forces. In the German Army a panzer division was a mixture of all arms—tanks, artillery, infantry, antitank guns—used to working in close cooperation. Rommel could shift his mobile forces anywhere on the battlefield without having to worry about them being out of balance. This could not be done so easily in the Eighth Army. Not only did the separate services—artillery, infantry, armor—jealously guard their independence, but Cunningham had a wide assortment of nationalities to deal with. Indians, Australians, Englishmen, New Zealanders, and South Africans had different military habits, and they did not always mesh smoothly when thrown together in an emergency.

The armies differed too in their handling of armor. The tank had been introduced in World War I by the British (with Winston Churchill as one of its chief developers). "Nothing so revolutionary in effect had occurred in warfare since the utilization of the horse, back in the mists of antiquity," wrote the British military historian B. H. Liddell

IMPERIAL WAR MUSEUM, LONDON

Hart. Britain lost her lead between the wars, however, and by World War II, lagged badly in tank tactics. Her generals tended to put armor into action piecemeal and to try to bull their way through defenses with tanks alone.

German armored commanders such as Rommel saw that tanks were at their most lethal against "thin-skinned" enemy forces—supply columns, infantry formations, artillery positions. The real counter to the tank was the antitank gun rather than another tank, and Rommel used these guns on offense as well as defense. If he could manage it, he would assault enemy armor with his antitank guns right up with his tanks in the line of advance; with the enemy tanks knocked out by these guns, his own tanks would be free to flail at the unguarded enemy infantry and supply services.

Operation Crusader was to jump off at dawn on November 18, 1941. Cunningham's forces moved into position the night before in a thunderstorm, the tanks and guns slithering through the mud, the infantry huddled together in their trucks against the cold, driving rain. All the next day the Eighth Army, over 100,000 strong, advanced across the empty desert under lowering storm clouds. There was no enemy to be seen. Committed to a battle plan based on what Rommel would do, Cunningham grew uneasy.

Rommel did not react because for once he had been sur-

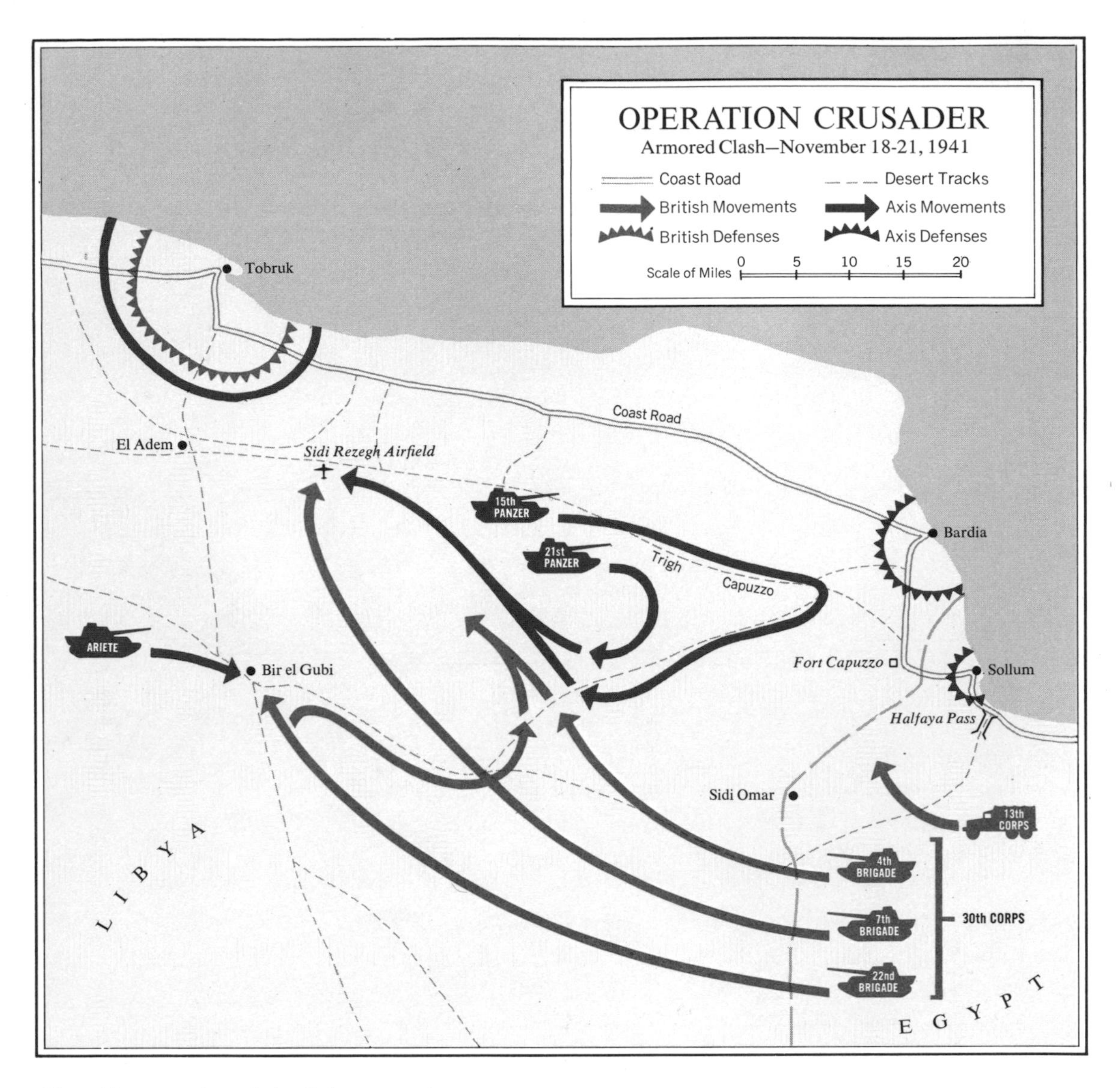

The wide separation of the British armored units in Crusader is traced on this map. After Rommel's panzer divisions, shown in gray, clashed with the 4th and 22nd brigades on November 20 (center), the Afrika Korps raced for Sidi Rezegh and hit the 7th Brigade before the rest of the British armor caught up.

prised. British security and camouflage had been good enough to prevent German Intelligence from seeing the massing of the Eighth Army. In addition, Rommel was preoccupied with an offensive against Tobruk that he had scheduled for November 21.

The 30th Corps initially advanced around Rommel's flank with only two of its three armored brigades; the third was held back to help protect Godwin-Austen's infantry corps. Then, on November 19, the British armor became further divided. While the 7th Armored Brigade seized the Sidi Rezegh airfield, an important point that endangered Axis communications between Tobruk and the frontier, the

22nd Armored Brigade was off to the south, skirmishing with the Italians, and the 4th Armored Brigade was off to the east, embroiled in a sharp fight with a probing column from the Afrika Korps. Thoroughly alert now, Rommel prepared to throw his two panzer divisions into the battle.

November 20 was a day of march and countermarch and confusion as the generals tried to sort things out. Groping for the enemy, Afrika Korps commander Cruwell ran one of his panzer divisions out of fuel. By late afternoon, however, he had tracked down General Alec Gatehouse's 4th Armored Brigade. For the second evening in a row, Gatehouse threw his American-built Honeys against the panzers and lost 26 of them. The 22nd Armored Brigade hurried back from its advanced position to help, but darkness put an end to the fighting.

On the fourth day of Crusader the mood of the British high command ranged from elation to bewilderment. Early in the morning Cruwell's panzers were seen to head off westward at high speed. As the 4th and 22nd armored brigades moved after them, Cairo headquarters flashed the news to the world that Rommel's army was in full retreat. The next day American newspapers reported that half the German tanks were destroyed and that the panzer divisions were "pocketed" and their situation "appears desperate."

The British tankers of the 7th Armored Brigade had a rather different view of the matter. They were holding Sidi Rezegh airfield, only ten miles from the Tobruk siege lines, and Rommel saw this position as the key to the developing battle. The Afrika Korps, far from retreating, was coming down hard on the 7th while holding off the two other slowly pursuing British armored brigades with a rear guard of antitank guns.

Attacking with antitank guns in the van, the two panzer divisions began chewing up the 7th Armored Brigade. British infantry major Robin Hastings watched as an enemy column approached the airfield over the rim of an escarpment. Five Crusader tanks rushing up to meet it were set aflame by antitank guns before their own 2-pounders came within range. Three British antitank guns then took up the fight. "We watched these three guns firing away," recalled Major Hastings, "watched the crews, completely composed, completely undaunted, picked off one by one." When the Afrika Korps finally broke off, short of gasoline and ammunition, the gallant 7th Armored Brigade had only 28 tanks left—but it still held Sidi Rezegh airfield.

For the next 48 hours Sidi Rezegh and the area around

German Stuka dive bombers, photographed over Libya in November of 1941 during the Crusader battle.

INCIDENT AT SIDI REZEGH

The speed and confusion of armored warfare can be glimpsed in this account by Robert Crisp, a South African who before the war had been an internationally known cricket star. It is from his book Brazen Chariots. *On November 27, 1941, the tenth day of the Crusader battle, Crisp's squadron of Honey tanks surprised a convoy of German supply trucks on a desert track called the Trigh Capuzzo, near Sidi Rezegh.*

The Honeys positively leaped over the top of the ridge and plunged down the steady incline to the Trigh. We were half-way down the slope and going like bats out of hell in the bright sunlight before the Jerries realized what was happening. Then the familiar pattern of alarm and confusion and panic-flight away from us at right angles to the road. . . .

Within seconds the dust was full of the crisscross pattern of tracers drawing red lines through the yellow cloud and puncturing the fleeing dark shapes with deadly points. From the turret tops we let go with tommy-guns and revolvers, and every now and again the whip-crack of the 37mm interjected the staccato chatter of the Browning [machine gun]. I could still see a Honey or two racing alongside, but what was happening beyond the narrow limits of vision I could only guess.

Suddenly, through the dust, I saw the flat plane of the ground disappear into space. I yelled like mad at the driver to halt. He had seen the danger only a fraction of a second after I had, and jerked back on the brakes even while I was shouting at him. The tracks locked fast and we skidded to a violent stop with the front sprockets hanging over a sharp drop that started the descent of a steep escarpment. . . .

I became aware of an astonishing scene at the foot of the escarpment, where it leveled out into a broad wadi. Vehicles of all shapes and sizes were everywhere—some upright and still moving away as fast as they could; others stationary and bewildered; many lying on their sides or backs with the wheels poking grotesquely upwards. Dark figures of men darted wildly about.

Even as I watched, a great lorry went plunging down the escarpment out of control; it struck some outcrop and leaped high into the air somersaulting to the bottom in a fantastic avalanche of earth, rock, and scrub and odd-shaped bundles of men interspersed with jagged pieces of wood and metal. The concentration of transport in the wadi below was a wonderful target. I said quickly into the mouthpiece: "Both guns. Fire with everything you've got. . . ."

Suddenly there was a fearful bang, and simultaneously I was drenched from head to foot with an astonishing cascade of cold water. For a moment or two I was physically and mentally paralyzed. I just could not believe that anything like that could happen. Then realization came swiftly and terribly—the water tins on the back of the tank had been hit. It could mean only one thing. As I looked backwards I was already giving the order to the gunner to traverse the turret as fast as he bloody well could.

In one flash I saw it all, and the fear leaped in me. Not fifty yards away a 50mm antitank gun pointed straight at the Honey, pointed straight between my eyes. Beyond it were other guns and the sight I had dreaded most—a number of motionless Honeys and the huddled figures of our black-bereted men crouched on the sand or stretched out in the agony of death.

It took less than a second for the whole scene and its awful meaning to register in my mind. I could see the German gunners slamming the next shell into the breech as the turret whirled. I yelled, "Machine gun, fire!" In the same moment I saw the puff of smoke from the antitank gun and felt and heard the strike on the armor plating. Quickly I looked down into the turret. A foot or two below me the gunner was staring at his hand, over which a dark red stain was slowly spreading. Then he gave a scream and fell groveling on the floor. In the top right hand corner of the turret a jagged hole gaped, and through it, like some macabre peepshow, I could see the gun being reloaded. . . .

IMPERIAL WAR MUSEUM, LONDON

Eighth Army tankers put their new American-built Honeys through their paces before Operation Crusader.

I leaned down and pulled the trigger of the Browning, and kept my finger there until the gun jammed. God knows where the bullets went. Twice I felt the Honey shudder and the second time more water came pouring in. When the Browning stopped and my mind leaped about searching for some way to stay alive I suddenly saw the slim chance. If the tank would move at all, we could drop over the edge of the escarpment, we would be out of sight of those blasted antitank guns. I said urgently into the mike: "Driver, advance. Over the edge. Quick!"

I felt the gears engage, and for a split second the world stood still. Then the engine revved, and the Honey heaved forward and dropped with a violent crash over the escarpment. In the turret we were hurled about like corks, and then the bouncing stopped and we rode smoothly down the slope. . . .

So much had happened in a few minutes, or a few hours it might have been, and I had looked so closely into the valley of the shadow, that I found it difficult to return to reality. I just could not fully absorb our situation. . . . We were chugging along casually through the deserted silence of the wadi. It was uncanny after the tumult and terror just behind us. . . .

The unreality persisted when the Honey swung right in response to my order, and moved slowly up the slope to the crest. As soon as my eyes were above the lip of the escarpment we halted, and the full picture of horror burst on me immediately.

Not much more than 500 yards away, like a projection on a cinema screen, lay the battlefield. My eyes lifted to the tall black columns, leaning slightly with the wind, and followed them down to the Honeys gasping smoke. Four of my tanks were blazing infernos; three others just sat there, sad and abandoned. A line of antitank guns with their crews still manning them expectantly, lined the edge of the drop. The whole scene was silhouetted sharply against the yellow clouds of dust which rose in a thick fog from the wadi below. I could see many men running about between guns and tanks and vehicles. My heart ached as I picked out the familiar bereted figures of our own troops, huddled in disconsolate groups or being shepherded singly by gesturing Germans. . . .

it was the scene of a savage, chaotic struggle. The airfield was strewn with disabled tanks and burned-out trucks, and the air was fogged with smoke and the dust churned up by thousands of vehicles. Supply columns snaked their way around the fringes of the ever-widening battle to feed fuel and ammunition to the fighters.

Neither high command was able to get a clear picture of what was going on. Often leadership came from officers of lower rank who led from "up front" by personal example. Captain Heinz Schmidt of a German rifle regiment wrote of directing a mixed panzer force against a South African position near the airfield on November 23. One after another the staff cars leading the charge were shot up and their officers killed; finally, only Schmidt was left alive, lying wounded in a slit trench, despairing over the failure of the advance. Then a young lieutenant came forward, rallied the leaderless force, and led it straight through the South Africans.

Before long, exhaustion and confusion began to exact their toll. When the Germans finally overran Sidi Rezegh airfield, a British officer watched through binoculars as a column of dispirited, totally exhausted German infantrymen occupied the field, and thought they looked more

In the fighting at Sidi Rezegh, wrote Alan Moorehead, "the hard, armored coating of both armies was destroyed. The softer, slower infantry was . . . left to decide the battle." Here, British soldiers dash by a battered German tank.

IMPERIAL WAR MUSEUM, LONDON

like sleepwalkers than victors. Another officer confessed: "I can truthfully say that none of us had more than the vaguest idea where we were from day to day and hour to hour, or what was happening either to our own forces or the enemy's."

Robert Crisp of the 4th Armored Brigade told how the fight for Sidi Rezegh airfield looked to a tank commander in the thick of it. "Twelve hundred yards ahead of me," Crisp wrote, "stretched the array of dark brown shapes, 60 or 70 monsters in a solid line abreast coming steadily towards the landing ground. The vicious flashes at the end of their gun muzzles stood out in fearful contrast against their camouflage. Behind them the sky was blood-red.

"I picked up the mike to speak to the gunner: 'Cannon. Twelve hundred. . . . Pick out one and stay on it till you knock it out. Get cracking!' I heard the first shot go off almost immediately and watched the tracer sail in a long shallow curve. It hit on one of those dark silhouettes and bounded high into the air. We were much too far out of range to do any great damage, but I had to do something. . . .

"The air was full of lead and noise, and the tanks crept towards me with their guns belching. Mingled with the detonations of the high explosive shells and my own cannon I could hear that terrifying swish of armor-piercing shells and sometimes get a split-second glimpse of a tracer going by, taking the breath out of my lungs with the vacuum of its passage. Every now and again my Honey would give that quick lurch which meant a hit.

"I heard my gunner yell 'I've got one, sir!' and it sounded good to hear his elation and to see the slow smoke curling up from the Mark III and the men bail out. The gunner was all right. . . . The loader was all right too. He would be too busy to be scared—tugging the next shell out of its bracket, pulling down the ejection lever, whipping in a new shell with enough force to close the breech, bending under to tap the gunner in the 'gun ready' signal, and then starting all over again. . . .The driver was the chap I felt sorry for. He would be squeezed back and to one side, getting as far away from his driving slit [in the armor] as possible, inactive and frightened to death. . . .

"I had a last despairing search behind me for some sign of rescue and support, and then I decided to go. . . . I said as quietly as I could into the mike: 'Gunner, cease fire. Driver, advance—turn about—go like hell!'

"That 'driver, advance' was the critical moment. It was

CAPTURED GERMAN RECORDS, NATIONAL ARCHIVES

An Afrika Korps tank captain and his radioman refresh themselves. General Rommel, an avid amateur photographer, took this picture.

The aftermath of Operation Crusader: two Afrika Korps tanks and a supply truck in flames on the battlefield. The Panzer Mark III in the foreground, like most German tanks, has pieces of tank track welded to the front

IMPERIAL WAR MUSEUM, LONDON

of its hull to act as additional armor. All told, the Germans and Italians lost about 330 tanks during the battle, and the Eighth Army lost over 600, although both sides managed to recover and repair perhaps half their derelicts.

BOTH: CAPTURED GERMAN RECORDS, NATIONAL ARCHIVES

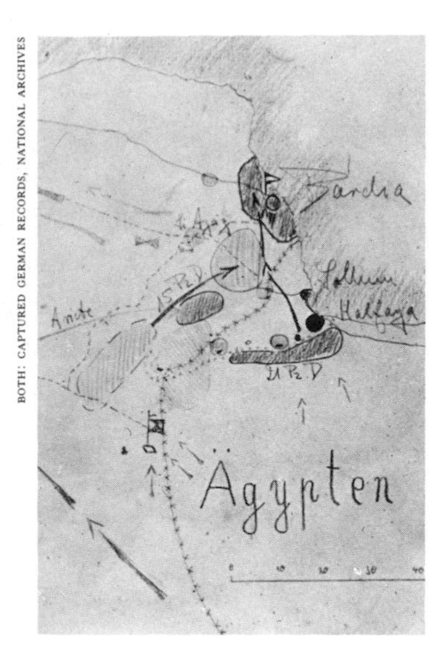

The map above, sketched by Rommel, shows the Afrika Korps' position on November 26 during its raid far behind Eighth Army lines. The 15th and 21st panzer divisions are labeled moving toward Bardia. The Afrika Korps withdrew the next day, its raid a failure. Below, Rommel inspects a map held by an aide.

always the same after a slugging match with the enemy; that frantic second of time when you did not know whether the tank would move or not. Even if the engine is still running, the suspension may be blasted; either of the tracks may be lying on the sand in mangled pieces; any of those sickening lurches might have meant the end of your last hope—mobility. I held my breath and felt the tank heave as the gears engaged. Then the engine seemed to rev high with relief, and the tank moved forward. . . .

"We got round the turn-about without disaster, and soon we were speeding back across the airfield, jinking left and right, creating our own smoke screen of dust. . . . So we fled back, running that incredible gantlet of death, each second beckoning us to safety. . . ."

The testing of men in war is cruel and searching, and one of the things that separates the great general from the merely good one is a relentless probing for an opposing commander's weakness. On the night of November 23 General Cunningham at Eighth Army headquarters believed he had lost the tank battle upon which Operation Crusader hinged. Some 300 of his cruisers had been knocked out; as far as he could see, withdrawal to protect his "thin-skinned" infantry was his only choice.

Rommel had measured Cunningham by the way he conducted his battle, and had found him wanting. "What difference does it make if you have two tanks to my one," Rommel was to tell a captured British officer after the battle, "when you spread them out and let me smash them in detail? You presented me with three brigades in succession!" With a sixth sense for reading his opponent's mind, he conceived a stroke that violated military logic but was well calculated to press Cunningham into retreat. At midmorning on November 24, with all his armor (the Afrika Korps had only 90 tanks remaining), Rommel left the battlefield entirely and raced eastward to the Egyptian border, seeking to wreck the Eighth Army's communications and supply lines and overrun its infantry.

What Rommel did not know, however, was that the man he was aiming at no longer held the power of decision. Matters were now in the hands of General Auchinleck. The commander in chief had flown from Cairo to Eighth Army headquarters the night before to be briefed on the crisis and to listen to Cunningham's recommendations. Claude Auchinleck was a big, powerful, decisive man with strong opinions and a wide stubborn streak. He realized that Rommel too had suffered heavily; outnumbered from the first, the Germans could ill afford their losses. He refused to approve a retreat. The next morning, as the Afrika Korps was setting off for the frontier, he sent a curt directive to Cunningham: "You will . . . continue to attack the enemy relentlessly, using all your resources even to the last tank."

Auchinleck's decision—certainly as bold a gamble as Rommel's raid—was eventually to turn the tide of battle. The German panzers were successful in "clipping the tail" of the Eighth Army, and they came very close to stumbling on the two huge supply dumps upon which the whole army depended. War correspondent Alan Moorehead, who was with the supply units caught up in the raid, called it a

On their dash to the frontier, Rommel's two panzer divisions just missed the main Eighth Army supply dumps, were blocked by the British 13th Corps, then had to retreat to help stop the breakout of the Tobruk garrison (upper left).

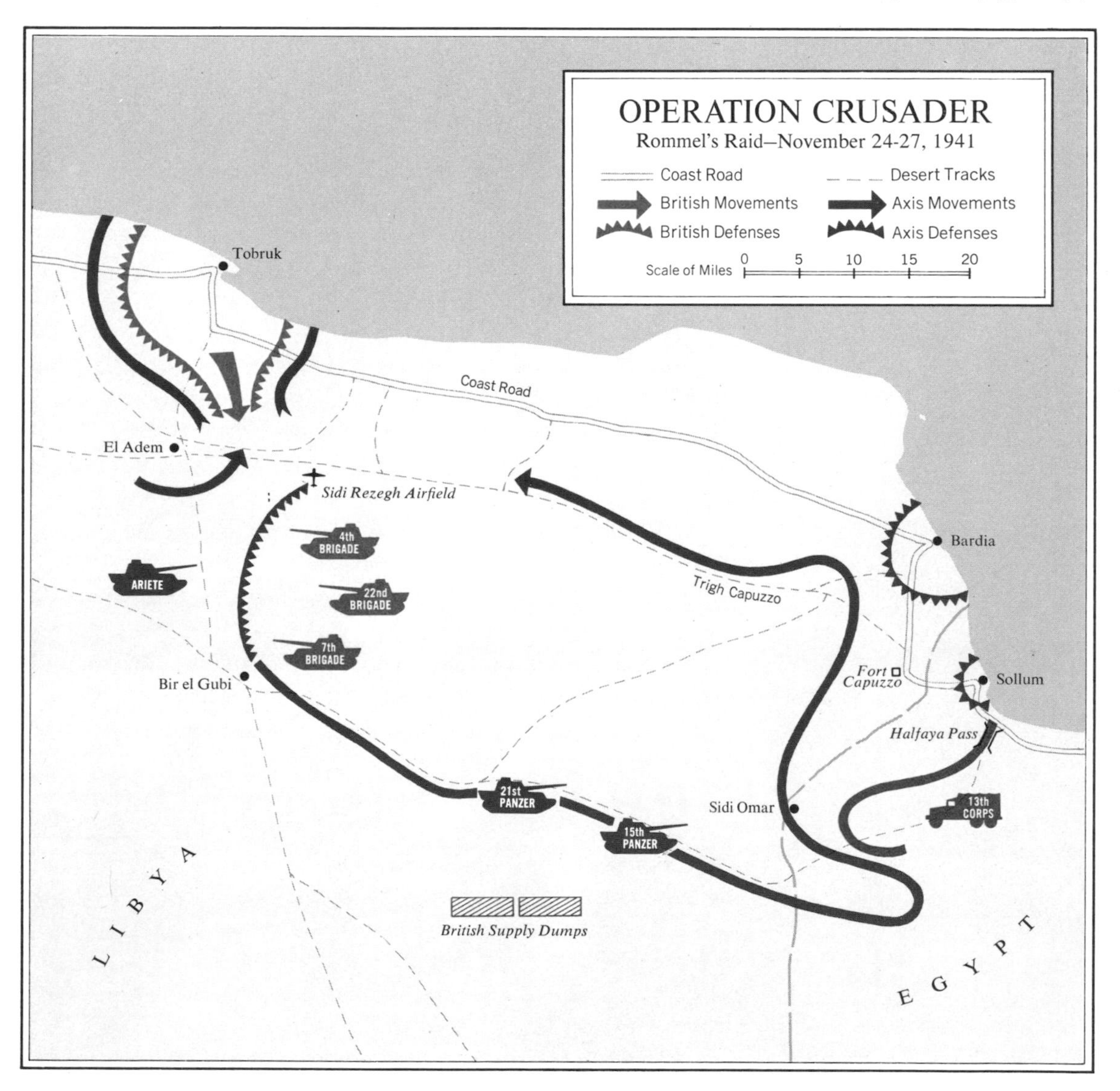

BOTH: IMPERIAL WAR MUSEUM, LONDON

Winter rains hampered the British pursuit of Rommel following the Crusader battle. In this picture, taken in January of 1942, RAF airmen bail out after a storm.

stampede. "All day for nine hours we ran," he wrote. "It was the contagion of bewilderment and fear and ignorance." But because of Auchinleck's firmness, the British fighting forces were hardly affected. After indecisively milling about in the frontier area, the Afrika Korps had to return to aid its beleaguered infantry comrades at Sidi Rezegh.

The Crusader battle dragged on for ten more days, sometimes smoldering, sometimes flaring up brightly. General Cunningham was replaced as head of the Eighth Army by General Neil Ritchie, but by then the British brigade commanders had the bit in their teeth and ran the battle. Sidi Rezegh changed hands three times; slowly, however, superior strength and superior reserves began to tell. The Eighth Army and the Tobruk garrison linked up, and by December 7, Rommel was down to 30 tanks. He had to give up the battlefield, give up the siege of Tobruk, and retreat. (That same day, halfway around the world, Japan attacked Pearl Harbor; now Britain and America were full war partners.)

Correspondent Moorehead moved up with the advancing British and examined the Sidi Rezegh airfield, where so much of the Crusader fighting had taken place. Everywhere he saw graves marked with a helmet or a belt, some with simple crosses made from packing cases and bearing penciled names. "Sometimes there were mingled German and British graves," he wrote, "as though the men had gone down together, still locked in fighting. Sometimes the dead were laid alongside the blackened hulks of their burnt-out tanks. . . . You could see the mess boxes, the toothbrushes and blankets of the crews scattered around together with their little packets of biscuits, their water bottles, photographs of their families. . . . Like great lizards, the broken tracks of tanks were sprawled across the sand with their teeth gaping upward. . . . Over everything hung the bleak winter's sky."

Rommel continued to withdraw through Cyrenaica, steadily but without panic. On Christmas Eve the pursuing British occupied Benghazi. By early January, 1942, Rommel was at El Agheila, back where he had started nine months before. The Axis frontier positions at Bardia and Sollum, now completely cut off, had to surrender.

Crusader was unquestionably a British victory, for it achieved its goals—the relief of Tobruk, the destruction of the bulk of the German armor, the recapture of Cyrenaica. Yet there was little of the pride and elation that had greeted the Wavell-O'Connor victory over the Italians the winter before. Too many mistakes had been made, too much strength had been frittered away, too many men and machines had been lost needlessly. Rommel, the Desert Fox, had somehow managed to dominate the battle even in defeat.

An Eighth Army sergeant (left) brings in an Afrika Korps prisoner.

Rommel, in fact, refused to stay defeated. On January 17, 1942, he wrote his wife: "I'm full of plans that I daren't say anything about around here [to the Italian high command]. They'd think me crazy. But I'm not; I simply see a bit farther than they do. . . ." Four days later, his tank strength reinforced to about 100, the Desert Fox launched a counterstrike that took the British (and the German and Italian high commands as well) completely by surprise.

Driving his men hard as always, rapidly shifting the weight of his attack from one column to another, Rommel scattered the British formations facing him in Cyrenaica. He feinted his enemy out of Benghazi, capturing huge stocks of supplies and fuel to keep his offensive moving. In two whirlwind weeks the Eighth Army was again driven out of the Cyrenaican bulge and into a defensive position at Gazala, 35 miles west of Tobruk.

This counterstroke, beyond recapturing the port of Benghazi and the important Cyrenaican airfields, was more than anything else a moral victory. It enlarged even more the Desert Fox's reputation for invincibility; he might be checked, but he had yet to be defeated. It remained to be seen how much this reputation would weigh on the scales of future battles.

IV

DESERT CRISIS

For some three and a half months, early in 1942, an uneasy lull settled over the Western Desert. The two armies lay inert at Gazala, exhausted by their heavy losses in the winter battles, while in London, Cairo, Berlin, and Rome their masters debated grand strategy.

The Nazi blitzkrieg in Russia had bogged down as it met stiffening resistance and the frigid winter, and heavy arms shipments from Britain and the United States were helping to keep the Red Army alive. As he hatched plans for a renewed assault on Russia, Adolf Hitler looked once more at that grand scheme for a Middle Eastern pincers movement suggested a year before. This time he envisioned the lower jaw of such a pincers thrusting against Russia's vulnerable southern flank, perhaps even linking up with the Japanese advancing from the Far East. Two things stood in the way of such a strategy—the British Eighth Army at Gazala and the island of Malta in the Mediterranean.

Behind the desert battles raged the grim, unseen, unceasing battle of supply. The British supply line around Africa was 14,000 miles and six weeks long, yet it was relatively safe from attack. Rommel's lifeline stretched only from Italy and Sicily across the Mediterranean to Tripoli, but it was vulnerable to air and sea attack every mile of the way. Malta was the key. The small British island 60 miles south of Sicily armed the planes and submarines that harassed the Axis supply routes. The Royal Navy's only other bases were at Alexandria and Gibraltar, at opposite ends of the Mediterranean; the only other RAF fields were in

This water color of a British armored car on patrol duty in Cyrenaica is by A. A. Gregson. Such patrols, loaded down with gasoline, water, and equipment, prowled the desert flank of the two armies for days at a time.

IMPERIAL WAR MUSEUM, LONDON

Cyrenaica (when the British held that area, which in early 1942 they did not) and Egypt.

In April and May of 1942 the Luftwaffe set about removing Malta from Britain's Mediterranean chessboard. Wave after wave of bombers and fighters pounded the island. Air-raid sirens wailed at all hours of the day and night; in April the alerts averaged nine a day. Dockyards, supply depots, and airfields suffered heavily, and food stocks dipped perilously low. Twice in these desperate months the American aircraft carrier *Wasp* slipped secretly into the Mediterranean, made a high-speed dash eastward, and flew off RAF Spitfires to bolster the island's fighter defenses.

Malta survived, living mostly on a diet of stubborn courage, but its sting was gone. Axis convoys steamed safely across the Mediterranean to unload gasoline and tanks and guns for Rommel. For the only time in his North African

ULLSTEIN-BIRNBACK

In April and May, 1942, the Italian fleet delivered more than 235,000 tons of supplies to Axis forces in North Africa, its best delivery record of the desert war. At left, a Panzer Mark III is unloaded at Tripoli. At right, the U.S. carrier Wasp *carries 46 Spitfires to Malta in May. This was the* Wasp*'s second such trip, and Winston Churchill thanked her crew with the message "Who said a wasp couldn't sting twice?" In the background is the British carrier* Eagle.

campaigns, the Desert Fox got something close to the supplies he needed.

The Germans had drawn up plans to seize Malta, as they had seized the island of Crete the year before. But with the Luftwaffe's success, it was decided to let Rommel strike the first blow. He would open his Western Desert offensive in late May. If and when he reached the Egyptian frontier, he was to pause while Malta was taken. With that thorn removed from his side, the great campaign could resume.

As Malta's agony continued, Winston Churchill's short temper grew shorter still. In Russia the Nazi steamroller was beginning to gather speed again. In the Pacific and the Far East the Japanese advanced unchecked. At home Britons grumbled about the way the government was running the war. Since only in North Africa were the British at grips with the German Army, Churchill stepped up the pressure

U.S. NAVY PHOTO, NATIONAL ARCHIVES

In Charles Pears' painting above, a British supply convoy fights its way through a strong Italian battle fleet to reach Malta in March, 1942. Three camouflaged Royal Navy cruisers are visible at the right, left center, and far left. A smokescreen shields the merchant ships at far right. After reaching Malta, the convoy was mercilessly bombed, and only one fifth of its cargo was saved. The scene at right, by Hubert Freeth, was painted aboard a British troopship during the voyage around Africa.

IMPERIAL WAR MUSEUM, LONDON

IMPERIAL WAR MUSEUM, LONDON

on Auchinleck to attack, to win a desert victory and restore Britain's morale and prestige. Finally, on May 10, the pressure was put as a direct order. Plans for an early offensive, code-named Operation Buckshot, were prepared.

As strategy was hammered out in the war councils, the soldiers in the Western Desert, as soldiers everywhere have always done, sat and waited. The heat and the dust and the crawling flies did not make the waiting easy. Raw "desert sores," intestinal diseases, and plagues of sand fleas added to the torment. Off duty there was nothing to do and nowhere to go, except perhaps to the Mediterranean once a week for a swim.

The only thing more monotonous than the routine and the terrain was the army food. The Eighth Army staple was

BOTH: IMPERIAL WAR MUSEUM, LONDON

British war artist Anthony Gross sketched the inside of an Eighth Army command truck filled with communications equipment. Enemy radio "traffic" was carefully analyzed for clues about the location of units or for revealing remarks made "in clear" (not in code).

canned corned beef, or bully, that had all the flavor of sawdust. In the Panzerarmee Afrika, as Rommel's army was now named, the counterpart of bully was an Italian sausage labeled A.M. A.M.'s tough stringiness soon had the Germans calling it *Alter Mann*, or "old man." Italian soldiers were more candid—they called it *Asino Morte*, "dead donkey." Whenever either side captured the other's rations, of course, bully or A.M. suddenly became a delicacy.

No two armies ever went at each other more savagely in battle, yet between them there had gradually developed a bond, as close to a code of chivalry as the war produced. Perhaps this was because of their mutual dislike of the barren land they struggled for; perhaps it was the absence of secret police and concentration camps and conquered populations; or perhaps it was simply the decency of the generals who led both armies. Whatever the reasons, the war in North Africa saw few of the atrocities that stained other battlefields of World War II. Prisoners were not mistreated. Flags of truce were honored to remove dead and wounded after a battle, and doctors treated friend and foe impartially.

This bond also grew out of a shared stock of desert legends. Men on both sides chuckled over the time that the

In another Gross drawing, New Zealand infantrymen prepare for battle. If the desert was too rocky to dig foxholes, heaped-up stones, or "sangers," gave some protection. In the background are American-built Grant tanks, used for the first time in the Gazala battle.

Long Range Desert Group popped up miles from nowhere and made off with the drowsy Italian garrison of an oasis fort without a shot being fired; or the exploit of the German scout who appropriated a British military policeman's cap and directed an entire Eighth Army supply convoy up a side track and "into the bag." They recounted the tale of the British division commander who within 48 hours was captured twice and twice escaped and then spent an entire day hiding in a dry cistern while a tank battle raged around him; or of Rommel suddenly appearing at a British field hospital at the height of the Crusader fight, inquiring about the welfare of the wounded and the stock of medicines, and then driving off again before the startled staff realized how easily they could have captured him. And every night at ten o'clock, radios all over the desert were turned on, and Allied and Axis soldiers alike sat quietly and stared across the dark landscape and thought of home as they listened to a European short-wave station serenade them with a sad and sentimental German ballad called "Lili Marlene."

As the weeks dragged by, the two armies slowly rebuilt their strength. General Ritchie's Eighth Army welcomed shipments of new tanks and new antitank guns. From

America came the Grant, a big, tall, awkward-looking tank that packed a heavy wallop. In addition to a 37-mm. gun in a revolving turret, the Grant had a powerful 75-mm. gun mounted in the hull. This gun had a limited field of fire—it was aimed by aiming the tank itself—yet it outranged and outhit any other tank gun on the British side. The new anti-tank gun was the 6-pounder, a 57-mm. weapon with good range and penetrating power. By May the Eighth Army had over a hundred 6-pounders, although their crews lacked the proper armor-piercing ammunition for them.

As for the Panzerarmee Afrika, its heavy tank losses in Crusader were made good during Malta's pounding. Rommel had 223 Panzer Mark III's with the short 50-mm. gun but with considerably thicker armor. He also had 19 of the new Mark III Specials, each mounting a long-barreled,

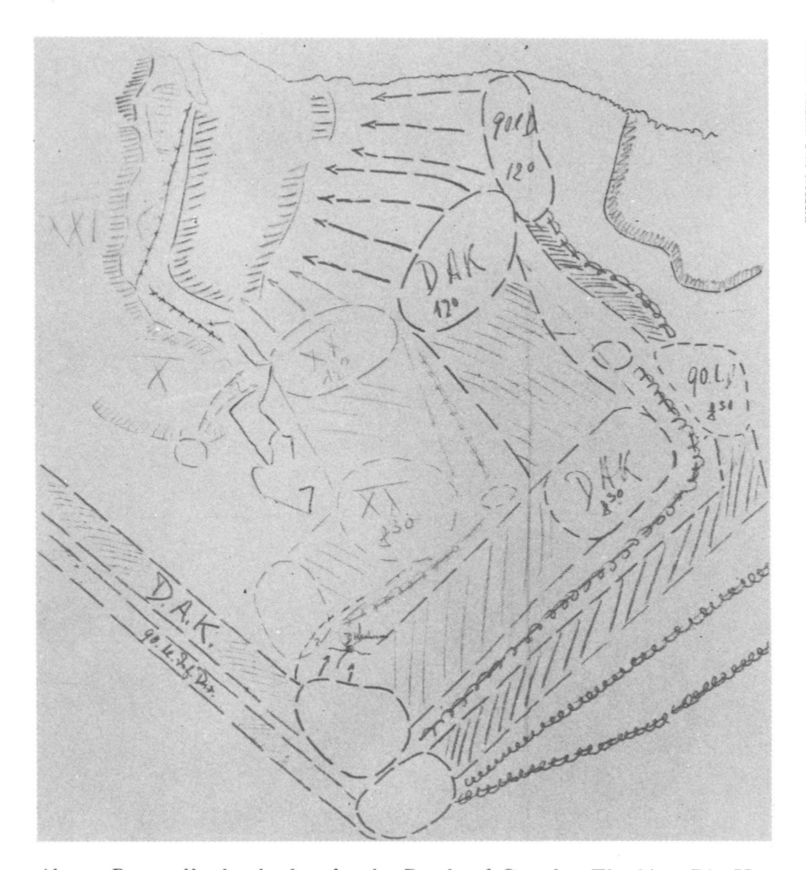

IMPERIAL WAR MUSEUM, LONDON

Above: Rommel's sketch plan for the Battle of Gazala. Flanking Bir Hacheim on the night of May 26, panzers of the DAK (Deutsches Afrika Korps) and the 90th Light Division (both in blue), plus the Italian XX Corps (green), were to be behind enemy lines by 8:30 the next morning and attacking the rear of the Eighth Army (red) by noon. Right: A. A. Gregson's painting of British guns in action at Gazala; a downed Stuka is at left.

high-velocity 50-mm. gun with half again the hitting power of the short gun of the same caliber. The tanks of the Italian Ariete armored division were little improved from the days of Marshal Graziani, and their embittered crews called them "self-propelled coffins." Rommel had a total of 560 tanks to Ritchie's 843 (including 167 American Grants), being outnumbered by three to two, but his antitank-gun strength was superior. The two air forces were about equal.

Ritchie could not get Operation Buckshot ready before June, 1942. Meanwhile, the Eighth Army lay stretched over some 40 miles of desert south of Gazala, arranged in heavily fortified "boxes" strung together by mine fields. The armored brigades were positioned behind this line. At nine o'clock on the evening of May 26, the detailed plans for Buckshot went into the trash barrel as Rommel struck first.

Under a bright moon, column after column of trucks and guns and tanks rolled forward. Some 10,000 vehicles strong, raising a towering cloud of dust, the Afrika Korps curled around Bir Hacheim, the southern anchor of Ritchie's Gazala Line. A British officer on patrol reported to headquarters: "Looks like a brigade of Jerry tanks coming." Then he looked again at the size of the dust cloud: "It's more than a brigade—it's the whole bloody Afrika Korps!"

For some reason Eighth Army headquarters was slow in getting and analyzing such reports. In the early daylight hours of May 27, Rommel pushed northward behind the

Any desert battlefield invariably became choked with dust; in this photograph, a German Panzer Mark IV gets directions. On its rear deck it has spare track and a wheel for its suspension system.

BOTH: IMPERIAL WAR MUSEUM, LONDON

The British high command in the Battle of Gazala. From left to right: Brigadier Erskine, a staff officer; General Willoughby Norrie of 30th Corps (armor); General Neil Ritchie, the Eighth Army's commander; and General "Strafer" Gott of 13th Corps (infantry).

Gazala Line, surprising some British units eating breakfast. Two motorized infantry brigades were scattered to the winds, and the headquarters of an armored formation was overrun. Yet despite these first successes, by afternoon the Afrika Korps was in deep trouble. The British put in uncoordinated but hard counterattacks, and Rommel had a third of his tanks knocked out; the long-range guns of the Grants came as a particular shock to the Germans.

May 28 was a day of confusion, with armored clashes flaring up at every point of the compass and a heavy sandstorm blanketing the battlefield. The Axis supply situation grew critical as truck convoys floundered on the long route around Bir Hacheim. As usual, Rommel was leading from up front, narrowly escaping injury in brushes with British columns and once being shelled by Italian artillery. That night he peronally led supply convoys to the stranded panzer divisions.

As the Battle of Gazala raged through its third day, and the British command continued to act sluggishly, Rommel decided to go over to the defensive temporarily in order to bind up his army's wounds. Instead of retreating, however, he lodged himself firmly in a nest of British mine fields in

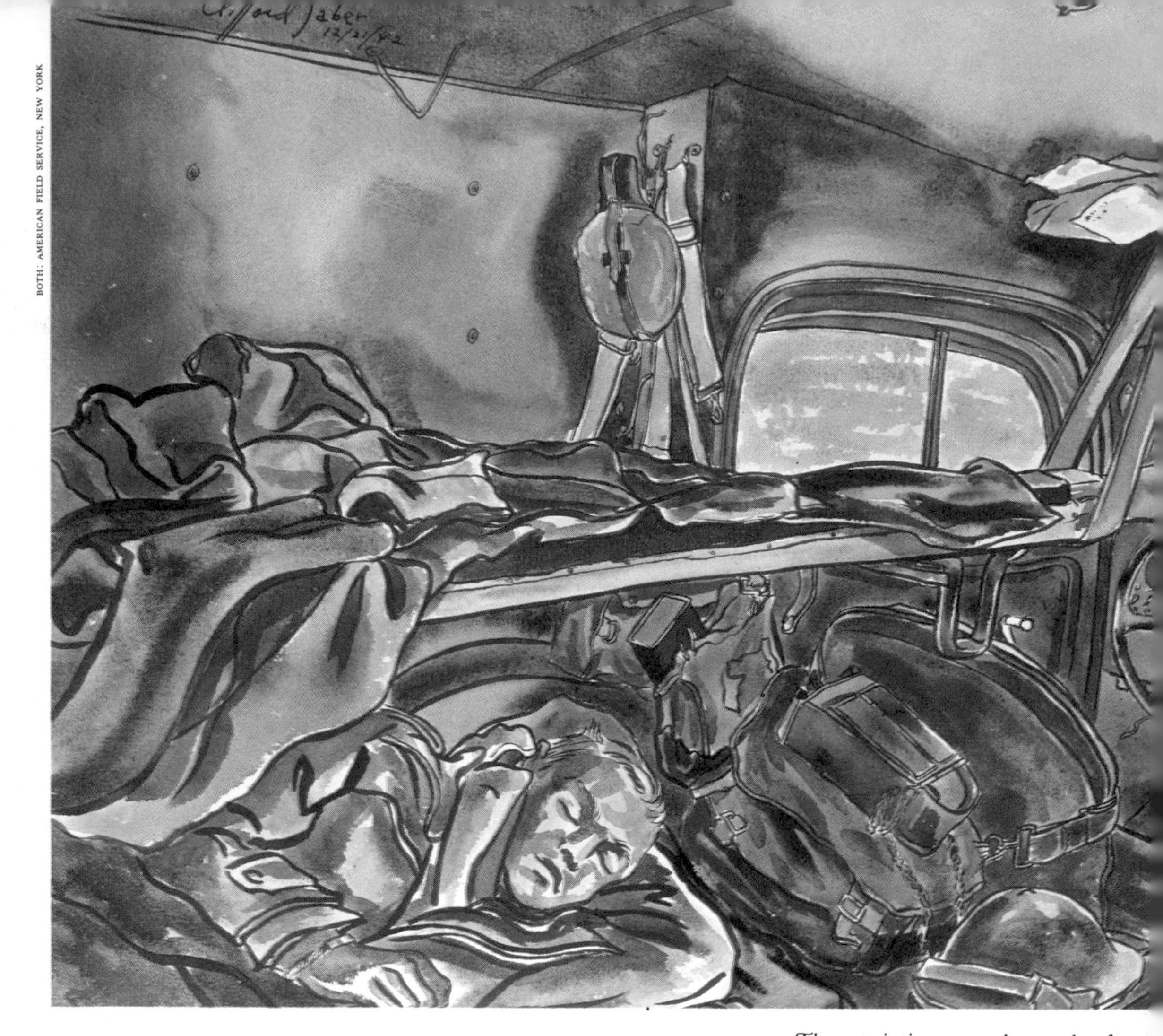

BOTH: AMERICAN FIELD SERVICE, NEW YORK

These paintings are the work of Clifford Saber of the American Field Service, who drove an ambulance for the Eighth Army. Above, a medical orderly naps in the back of an ambulance during a lull in the action. These ambulances carried four stretcher cases or as many as nine "walking wounded." At right is the operating room of a field hospital, sheltered by a tent fitted around the back of a supply truck. A cast is being put on the leg of a soldier wounded by the explosion of a land mine.

the center of the Gazala Line. Sappers (mine-removal crews) cut corridors through the mine fields at his back to open a direct route to his supply dumps and to the Italian infantry divisions facing the British in the north. Rommel's bridgehead came to be known as the Cauldron.

With this brilliant stroke the Desert Fox once more confounded his opponent. General Ritchie could find no easy way to cope with the Cauldron. A frontal attack on the massed Afrika Korps was not an appealing prospect. If he reached out beyond the Gazala Line to threaten Rommel's supply line, he would expose his own supply dumps to an armored strike from the Cauldron. Unable to decide what to do, Ritchie and his generals fell to bickering.

Quickly, Rommel set about consolidating his new position. Right in the center of it was the troublesome British 150th Brigade box, steadily shelling his supply corridors through the mine fields. While a screen of antitank guns

held off the British armor, Rommel threw his full weight at the 150th Brigade. It fought for more than two days, to the last round of ammunition, before it was overwhelmed.

By June 5, the tenth day of the battle, General Ritchie had evolved a plan: a frontal attack on the Cauldron. "If ever an operation resembled sticking one's arm into a wasp's nest, this did," concluded a historian of the battle. On paper the plan, code-named Aberdeen, was complex but promising; in practice, it was a disaster. Units advanced in the wrong place at the wrong time; infantry attacked unsupported by armor; armor was not backed by artillery. The two armored brigades involved lost 118 tanks, half their strength, and in the confusion an Indian infantry brigade was left stranded within the Cauldron. After driving the British armor away, Rommel attacked the Indians the next day, all but wiping them out.

A British gunner recorded the death agonies of Aberdeen. "The next attack came in very quickly," he wrote, "and soon German tanks had overrun the infantry battalion in the rear and were nosing about the burning vehicles. . . . Events moved quickly now, and amazing things happened as the fighting raged at close quarters. A sergeant of the reconnaissance regiment with what was left of his section leaped on a German tank, trying to ram hand grenades through the turret. They were killed to a man. The machine-gun fire was intense. . . .

"The doctor and his orderly worked unceasingly in a

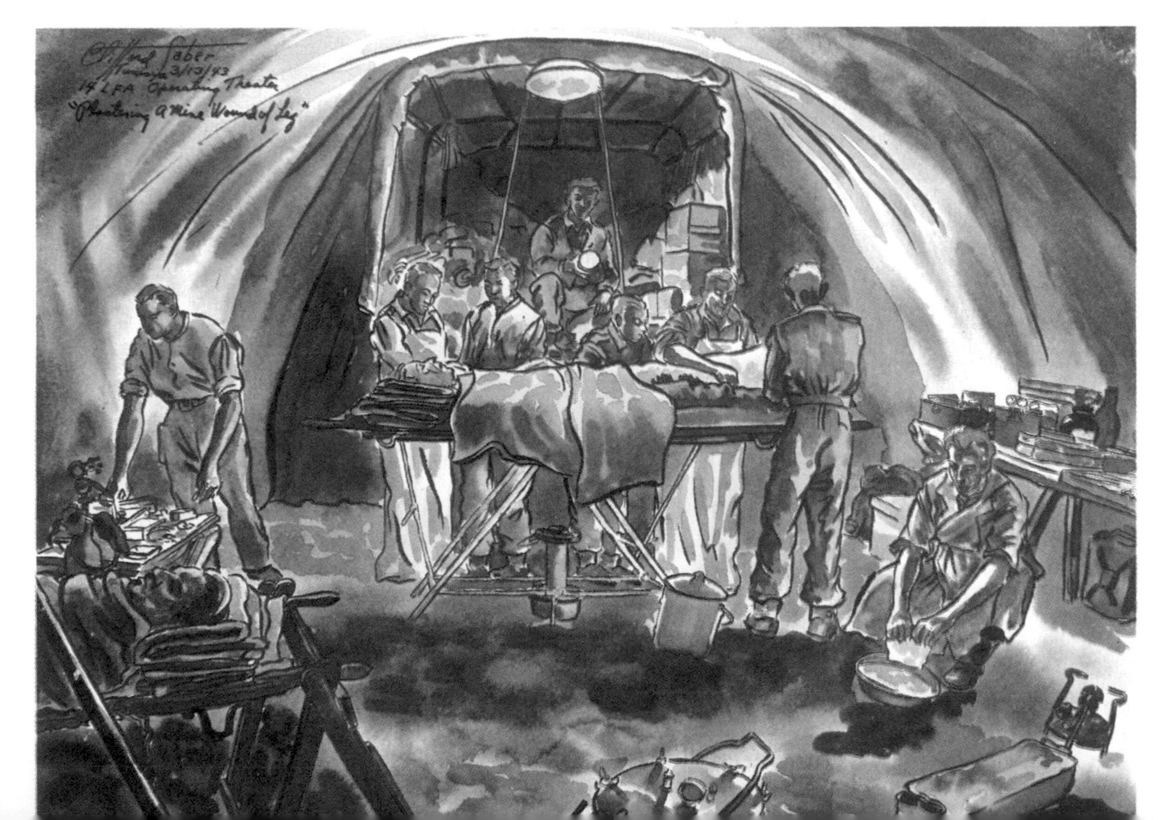

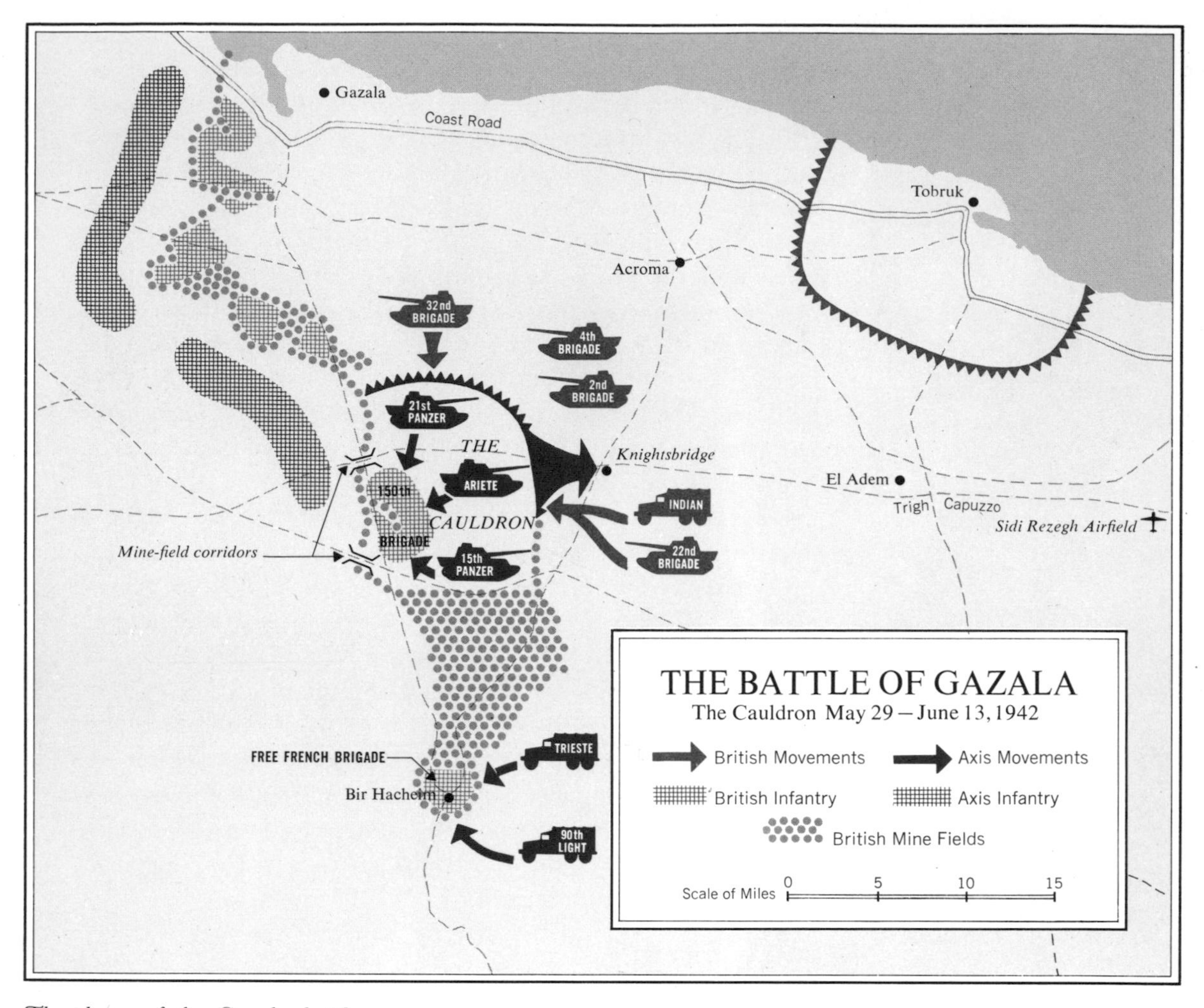

The phases of the Gazala battle centering around the Cauldron are shown here. First, Rommel consolidated his position in the Cauldron, eliminating the 150th Brigade, and opened supply corridors through the mine fields. Next, he repelled the attack of two British armored brigades and the Indian infantry. Third, the German 90th and the Italian Trieste divisions took Bir Hacheim. Finally, the massed Axis armor in the Cauldron struck east toward Knightsbridge.

murderous fire round the Command Post, which was a shambles of dead and wounded. . . . Of the antitank guns only one now remained, but there was no one to man it until a young lance-bombardier, with one arm blown off at the elbow, crawled out in a vain attempt to reach it. . . .

"The end was very near now. . . . The survivors of the battery turned sadly to their final task—the battering of their gun sights. For a few moments more the air sang with machine-gun bullets; then all was quiet, and that deep silence that descends on a battlefield when the contest is over spread over the Cauldron. . . ."

After his rout of Operation Aberdeen, Rommel turned his attention to a French garrison defending Bir Hacheim at the southern end of the Gazala Line. "Seldom in Africa was I given such a hard-fought struggle," he admitted. He led several assaults himself, and Luftwaffe Stukas dropped bomb after bomb into the defenses. Finally, the Frenchmen could hold out no longer, and on the night of June 10 the survivors broke out. All the while, the rest of the Eighth Army had "kept astonishingly quiet" (in Rommel's words), its high command seemingly paralyzed by the pace of events.

With his supply line secure and the southern half of the Gazala Line in his hands, the Desert Fox was ready to resume the offensive. The British line was now bent back at a right angle, with its hinge in an area known as Knightsbridge. On June 11 the Afrika Korps sprang out of the Cauldron toward Knightsbridge. Confused, disorganized, the British armored brigades were mauled one after another. The desert was strewn with derelict Crusaders and Grants and Stuarts, some of them only slightly damaged or out of fuel. But the British abandoned the field, and with them went any hope of recovering and repairing these casualties. On June 11 Ritchie reported a tank strength of 330; on the fourteenth he had 70. Knightsbridge became the blackest name in the Eighth Army's history.

There was nothing for Ritchie to do now but pick up the pieces and retreat. The only escape corridor left open for the British infantry in the northern part of the Gazala Line was the coast road passing through Tobruk. The Luftwaffe pitched into the columns of trucks and guns crawling eastward, and the "Gazala Gallop" began.

"Stragglers from other units cut in among the battalion transport and force the pace," begins a South African's account. "As the battalion vehicles try to regain their place, convoy discipline begins to go: a panicking few are breaking up the disciplined many. . . . The road is relentlessly machine-gunned and bombed. Trucks blaze. Men run; ambulances howl towards the hospital in Tobruk; dead men lie in blood and oil and broken glass. . . ."

By June 15 the Eighth Army was a beaten army, and Neil Ritchie was a beaten general. Rommel not only had a firm grip on the initiative but for the first time he had a substantial edge in tanks. That night he wrote his wife jubilantly, "The enemy is breaking up. . . . We've made a pretty clean sweep this time." The next stop, he vowed, was Tobruk.

To Rommel and Churchill, the two men who would decide its fate, Tobruk was more than anything else a symbol. No matter that despite the eight-month siege it had withstood in 1941 it was now militarily indefensible, its mine fields incomplete, its antitank ditches so full of drifted sand

ULLSTEIN-BIRNBACK

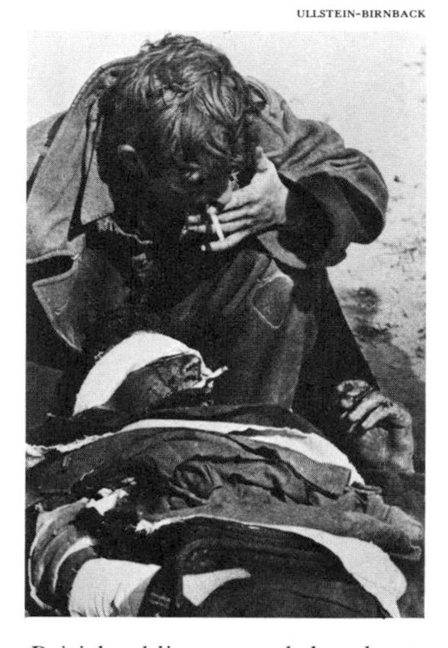

British soldiers wounded and captured during the Gazala Gallop.

that they "would hardly have interfered with the progress of a garden roller." No matter that its harbor facilities were far too slight to handle all the supply needs of the Panzerarmee Afrika on a drive to the Suez Canal. Rommel would not rest until he had conquered the fortress that had defeated him. The Prime Minister would not hear of its being abandoned. "Presume there is no question in any case of giving up Tobruk," he imperiously signaled Auchinleck on June 14.

Even as Auchinleck and Ritchie cobbled together a force to defend Tobruk, Rommel cut off the fortress and issued orders for an assault. Promptly at first light on June 20 more than 200 German and Italian aircraft unleashed a torrent of bombs on the defenses, and the massed artillery of the Afrika Korps added to the chorus of destruction. Moving up behind the curtain of shells, German shock troops and engineers cracked the outer defense line, capturing many stunned defenders in their underground bunkers. Then the tanks moved forward through the gap, Rommel leading the way.

By early afternoon the 15th and 21st panzer divisions were enveloping Tobruk's strong points one by one. At the vital King's Cross road-junction, Rommel stood straddle-legged on the roof of his armored command car watching the progress of the battle through binoculars as bewildered British prisoners streamed by him. By evening the 21st

ULLSTEIN-BIRNBACK

This German photograph shows dejected Britons and South Africans of the surrendered Tobruk garrison with one of their armored cars.

CAPTURED GERMAN RECORDS, NATIONAL ARCHIVES

Rommel and the driver of his armored command vehicle sample fruit taken from the Eighth Army. After Hitler promoted Rommel to field marshal, highest rank in the German Army, following the capture of Tobruk, the Desert Fox remarked to his wife, "I would rather he had given me one more division."

Panzer was in the streets of Tobruk itself. Just then a relief column sent out by Ritchie was at Sidi Rezegh. "In the distance to the north," wrote one of its officers, "straight in the direction of the fortress, a great black cloud began to rise. Many of us had seen that cloud before, the token over a year before of the impending surrender of the Italians. Now we knew that the dumps, the great oil tanks, the supplies accumulated for our offensive to Benghazi, had been set on fire. . . ."

Through a night lit fitfully by flares and noisy with the stutter of machine guns and the harsh grinding of tanks, Tobruk's commander, South African general H. B. Klopper, tried to organize a breakout. But there was too little time and too few trucks. "Situation shambles," he signaled Ritchie. "Terrible casualties would result," he said, if he continued the fight. Shortly after dawn on June 21 a white flag was raised over Klopper's headquarters.

More than 32,000 prisoners fell into Axis hands, and

some 2,000 vehicles; more important, 2,000 tons of precious gasoline were seized before the defenders could destroy it. German troops rooted happily through the captured stores, filling up on South African pineapple, Irish potatoes, English beer—just as the Australians had reveled among the Italian stores captured in Tobruk in January, 1941. Rommel did not pause to gloat. "Fortress of Tobruk has capitulated," he announced to his army. "All units will reassemble and prepare for further advance." Hitler immediately promoted him to the rank of field marshal.

The news was a great tonic to the German public. In Berlin a neutral Swedish newspaperman watched celebrating crowds and reported that he had not seen such gaiety there since the news of the fall of France in 1940. Winston Churchill was in the United States, meeting with President Roosevelt. He had just finished breakfast and had gone to join Roosevelt in the White House study. Without a word the President handed him a message telling of Tobruk's surrender. "This was one of the heaviest blows I can recall during the war," Churchill was to write later. "I did not attempt to hide from the President the shock I had received. It was a bitter moment. Defeat is one thing; disgrace is another. . . ."

As Rommel drove his army eastward once more, clucking officers from the German and Italian high commands reminded him that he was to halt until Malta was taken—his Luftwaffe support would be needed for the assault on the island. The Desert Fox stormed at them that the Eighth Army was ripe for plucking, as it might never be again. When Marshal Ettore Bastico, commander of all Axis forces in North Africa, issued him a direct order to halt, Rommel replied that he would "not accept the advice," and invited Bastico to dine with him in Cairo. Finally, Hitler had to intervene, remarking that "it is only once in a lifetime that the Goddess of Victory smiles." The pursuit would go on. Malta would not be assaulted.

"How can one describe the retreat of a modern army?" wrote British correspondent Denis Johnston. "The roaring, rattling caterpillar of battered trucks and dirty men—the great transporters shouldering broken-down tanks, the RAF recovery lorries towing wrecked aircraft, the field kitchens and the ambulances . . . this mass of machinery churning the dust and spewing out petrol fumes, entangled in traffic blocks and then grinding onwards again. . . . Tractors and bulldozers—staff cars and clattering machine-gun carriers—armored control vehicles and map lor-

ALL: CAPTURED GERMAN DRAWINGS—U.S. ARMY

Wilhelm Wessel was in the North African desert so long that he became known as the official artist of the Afrika Korps. His sketch at upper left shows a knocked-out British "portee," a truck mounting a 2-pounder antitank gun, and its dead driver. The experimental portee was too conspicuous on the battlefield and was soon abandoned. Above, tankers check over a Panzer Mark III. The rack alongside the turret holds extra gas cans. At left is an Afrika Korps machine-gun crew at an outpost in Cyrenaica.

INCIDENT AT MATRUH

The Battle of Matruh, the climax of Rommel's 1942 campaign, was decided when the British armor withdrew. On the night of June 27–28 the 2nd New Zealand Division was ordered to break through the thin ring placed around it by the 21st Panzer Division. These excerpts describe the breakout. The first and third are from Infantry Brigadier, *a book by New Zealand's General Howard Kippenberger; the second account is by Lieutenant Colonel G. P. Hanna, taken from the history of the Royal Artillery.*

I was called to Division for a conference about eight o'clock that evening [June 27]. We stood in a group at the back of the command truck. Brigadier Inglis said that all attacks had been repulsed so far, but the enemy was fairly round behind us and we obviously were in a grave position. The going to the south was reported bad, the only sure going was due east, which meant that we must make a breakthrough. . . .

The trucks were packed to the limit and the hundreds of men whom they could not carry were crammed on to the fighting vehicles. Men were hanging on wherever there was standing room, squeezed inside the gun quads, on the guns themselves, on carriers and antitank gun haulers, everywhere imaginable. The loading was completed in a quiet and orderly manner and I walked round to check up. I found about twenty men still unaccommodated and they followed me round while I found places for them one by one. . . .

At last, well after midnight [writes Colonel Hanna], we started to move forward, the column led by the Royal Artillery brigadier. The 4th Brigade had not completed its attack, but we were forced to begin the breakout so that we should have a long enough period of darkness in which to get well clear of the enemy. We passed slowly through 4th Brigade's old area. There was little small-arms fire ahead of us, and later we learned that 4th Brigade had done tremendous execution with the bayonet.

We had gone only a short distance past the original forward posts when the scouting carriers moving just ahead of the column halted. A moment later the darkness in front exploded into fire. Tank shells and machine-gun bullets poured into the column, and a number of our vehicles burst into flames, illuminating the whole area.

We remained halted in reality for only a few seconds, uncertain what to do. Then the brigadier roared out from his jeep, "Follow me!" Several of us in the leading vehicles did so, and we drove hard right, that is, south, skirting the enemy tanks. The whole column followed. The going was poor, but any thought of cautious driving was abandoned. We had gone about 500 yards when more enemy tanks immediately in front of us opened fire. We halted again, and our predicament was obviously much more serious this time. Many of the leading vehicles went up in flames, a single shell in some cases going through two or three trucks in line.

My recollections are a little vague at this point; but I remember that, with no alternative, we started up and drove straight into the enemy's fire. I can well imagine the feelings of those tank crews when they saw an irresistible tide of vehicles and guns bearing down upon them. Trucks were still exploding in flames, but nothing could have halted that onrush, the product more of instinct than of command. The air was so heavy with dust and smoke that one could do nothing but follow the vehicle in front into the thick blanket ahead. A number of unfortunate men were thrown off motorcycles or tossed out of trucks. Their death was certain, for vehicles behind had no chance of avoiding them. . . .

My car was jammed on all sides and could

IMPERIAL WAR MUSEUM, LONDON

A British supply convoy near Matruh endures an attack by the Luftwaffe during the Gazala Gallop in June, 1942.

not move [resumes Brigadier Kippenberger]. . . . A few seconds later I saw the truck ahead of us turning to the left, and beyond it quite clearly saw John Gray standing with his head through the roof of his car pointing in the same direction. "We'll give it a go, Ross" [the driver], I said. "Very good, sir," he replied, as polite as ever. We followed the trucks ahead, all bolting like wild elephants. For a few moments we ran on amid a pandemonium, overtaking and being overtaken by other frantic vehicles, dodging slit trenches, passing or crashing into running men, amid an uproar of shouts and screams. I recognized the men as Germans, pulled out my revolver and was eagerly looking out for a target when suddenly there was silence and we were running smoothly on level desert. We were through. . . .

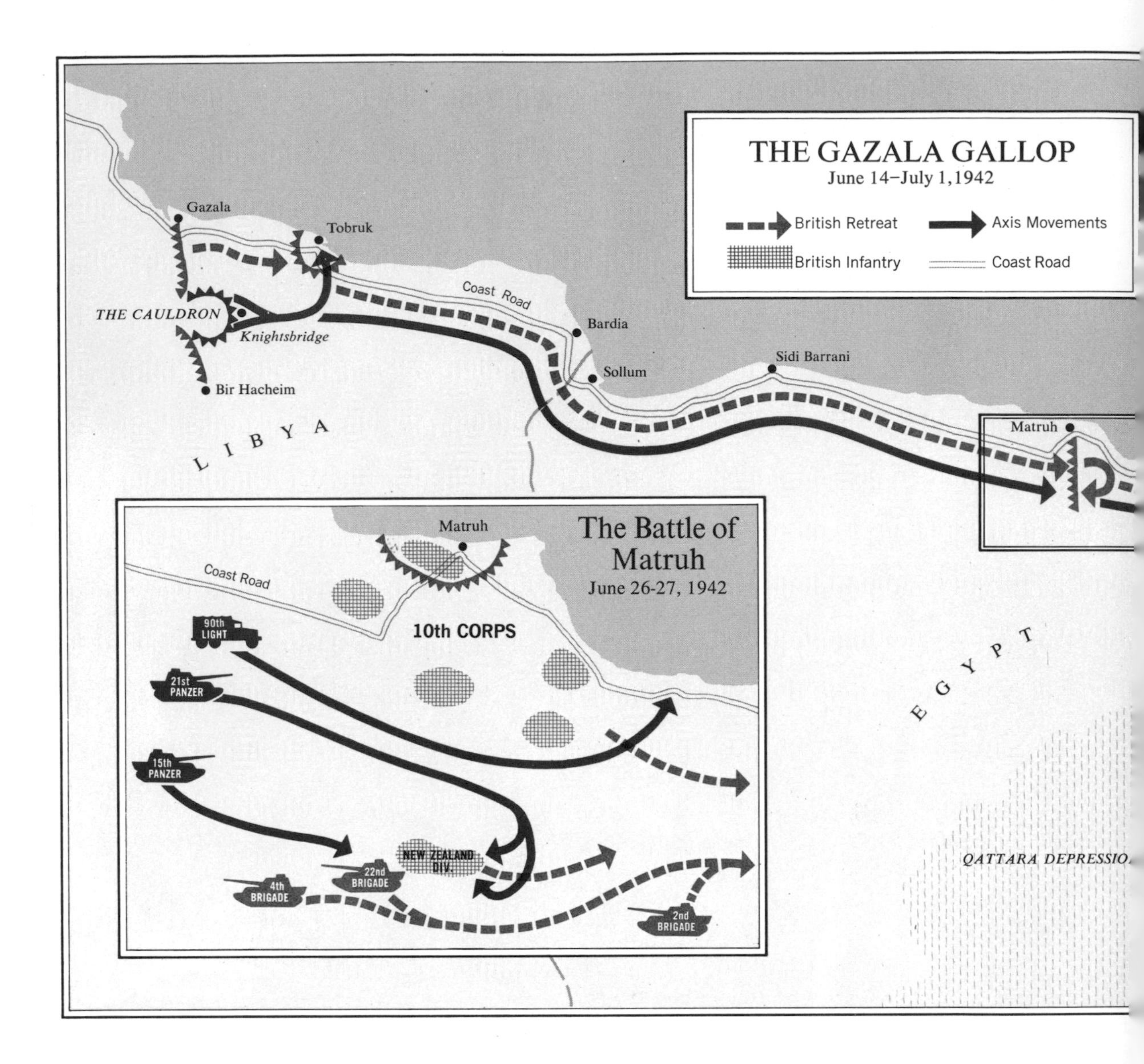

ries—trucks breaking off from the column and bumping violently across the margins of sand and scrub, followed by long trails of brown dust—trucks lining up for petrol—trucks in their tens and in their hundreds and in their thousands clanging and roaring their way eastward. . . ."

On June 23, two days after Tobruk's fall, the Panzerarmee reached the Egyptian frontier. The two German armored divisions had 44 tanks between them, the Italians 14 more. Infantry units were at skeleton strength, totaling about 2,500 German and 6,000 Italian. Four out of every five trucks were British, running on captured fuel. But Rommel's domination of his enemy was virtually complete.

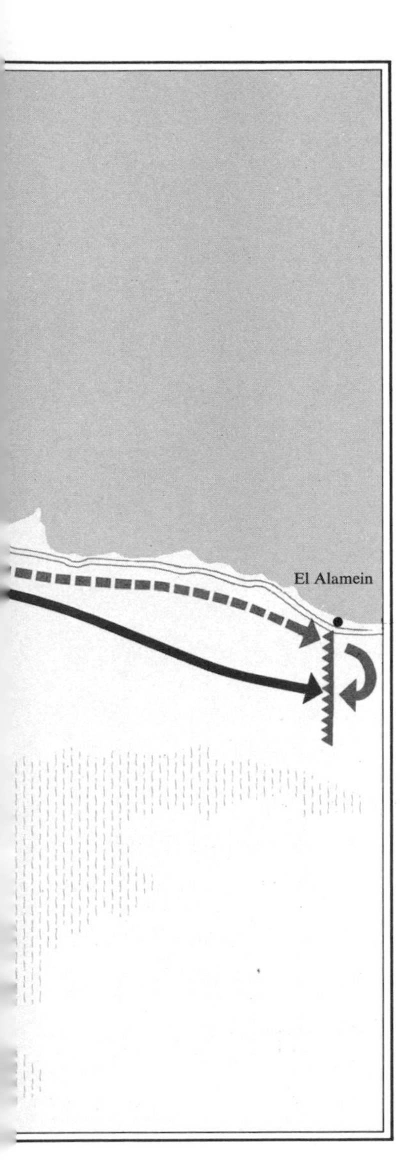

The Gazala Gallop began with the smashing of the British armor at Knightsbridge (upper left) and ended some two weeks later at El Alamein, 400 miles to the east. At the Battle of Matruh (inset) Rommel narrowly missed death or capture in a night action.

Ritchie could think of nothing but "to gain time with distance." His goal was a defensive position at Matruh, 120 miles inside the frontier. He arrived there on June 25, with Rommel nipping at his heels.

As Ritchie disposed his forces for battle, he announced that the retreat was over, that the Eighth Army would make its fight at Matruh and die there if it lost. That evening General Auchinleck, as he had done in the Crusader battle seven months before, flew up from Cairo and took over command of the army. Matruh was not where the Eighth Army would win or die, he decided. It must remain "in being" no matter how far it had to retreat if there was to be any hope of saving the Middle East.

Auchinleck had no time to make his presence felt before Rommel attacked. The Battle of Matruh was surely the most astonishing of the Desert Fox's career. Late on June 26 he drove what was left of the Afrika Korps through a nine-mile gap between the halves of the Eighth Army. The next day he resumed the advance, leaving the 90th Light Division, reduced to 1,600 men, to mask the entire British 10th Corps in Matruh. The panzer divisions tangled with some 150 British tanks assembled to the south.

The fighting was inconclusive, and by dusk the Afrika Korps was in a perilous position. The 90th Light lay isolated on the coast road east of Matruh, "cutting off" five full brigades of British infantry. The 21st Panzer Division, with 14 tanks and 600 infantrymen, "surrounded" a fresh New Zealand division just brought up from the Nile delta. The 15th Panzer Division, 20 tanks strong, was off to the west, facing two brigades of British armor.

British Intelligence, however, credited Rommel with four times as many German tanks as he had; in addition, the Rommel legend was now in full bloom. British general "Strafer" Gott, who had been fighting in the desert since O'Connor's offensive in 1940, was deeply under the spell of the legend that day. He believed the battle had been lost, and he ordered the armor to withdraw. The Eighth Army's position collapsed like a house of cards. The New Zealanders, unsupported by any armor after Gott's withdrawal, broke through the encircling 21st Panzer that night in a wild melee. On the next night the 10th Corps in Matruh pushed aside the 90th Light and also broke out. The Afrika Korps collected some 6,000 prisoners, more than its own total manpower. The Gazala Gallop continued, the next stop El Alamein, 60 miles from Alexandria.

As June turned to July it seemed that the end was near

IMPERIAL WAR MUSEUM, LONDON

General Claude Auchinleck—known to the Eighth Army as the Auk—talks to his men at El Alamein in July, 1942, after their long retreat from Gazala. "There were no signs of panic," he wrote, "but there was terrible disorganization."

for the Allies in the Middle East. On June 29 Benito Mussolini flew to Cyrenaica to prepare himself for the victory parade he would lead through the streets of Cairo; he brought with him a great white charger to help provide the proper Caesar-like image. Panic played over Alexandria and Cairo like summer lightning. The Royal Navy hastily pulled out of its base at Alexandria and steamed through the Suez Canal to the safety of the Red Sea. Great clouds of smoke rose over military headquarters in Cairo as fluttering clerks (the Short Range Desert Group, combat soldiers called them) burned bales of secret documents. So great was the fall of charred paper from their bonfires that July 1, 1942, became famous as "Ash Wednesday."

Beneath these ripples of panic, however, the Eighth

Army was getting a grip on itself. There are no soldiers more stubborn than British soldiers, and they gradually came to see what Rommel had got away with at Matruh. Auchinleck stood alone by the coast road, watching the trucks and guns and tanks roll into the El Alamein position, and thought that the men were tired and angry but that basically their morale was good; what they needed most was leadership. On June 30 he issued an order to his troops: "The enemy is stretching to his limit and thinks we are a broken army. . . . He hopes to take Egypt by bluff. Show him where he gets off." It was a completely accurate reading of the situation.

The Panzerarmee Afrika was at the very end of its tether. Its main supply line stretched almost 1,400 miles to Tripoli. Malta was back in business smashing Axis convoys. In an around-the-clock maximum effort, the RAF was decimating its columns with bombs and bullets. And its men were dead on their feet. "Rommel has wonderful energy himself," a German prisoner said, "but he drives us too hard, and some of us can't take much more of this."

BUNDESARCHIV, KOBLENZ

Afrika Korps veterans—"Rommel's boys"—pose at El Alamein.

Through July the two armies slugged groggily at each other at El Alamein. Rommel and Auchinleck were no longer able to inspire their exhausted officers and men to that extra effort needed for victory; the two commanders, said an observer, "were full of fire, but could not keep the battle aflame." On both sides opportunities were missed, mistakes were made. In one attack a green armored brigade fresh from England was hit hard by antitank fire, blundered into an uncharted mine field, and lost 93 out of 104 tanks. The Italian Ariete Division let itself be surprised by the New Zealanders and lost nearly all its artillery. "Things are going downright badly for me at the moment," Rommel wrote his wife on July 17. "The enemy is using his superiority, especially in infantry, to destroy the Italian formations one by one, and the German formations are much too weak to stand alone. It's enough to make one weep."

The crisis was over, the high-tide mark reached. Rommel's brilliant campaign was history; at El Alamein in July, 1942, he lost the initiative. By personal strength and unswerving purpose, Claude Auchinleck had ended the Gazala Gallop. Rommel himself delivered the final verdict: "Although the British losses . . . had been higher than ours, yet the price to Auchinleck had not been excessive, for the thing that had mattered to him was to halt our advance, and that, unfortunately, he had done."

V

DECISION AT EL ALAMEIN

On August 3, 1942, Winston Churchill landed at Cairo after a one-stop flight from England in a Liberator bomber. The Prime Minister had decided to examine for himself what was wrong with the Eighth Army and its generals. In Cairo he saw a galaxy of top military and civilian officials from all over the Middle East. Then, wearing a pith helmet and his famous one-piece "jump suit" and clenching a long cigar in his bulldog jaw, he stumped up and down the El Alamein line in the broiling sun, talking to the troops and questioning their officers. Finally, he called for "drastic and immediate" changes in the Middle Eastern command.

Heading the list of the dismissed was General Auchinleck. Like Wavell before him, Auchinleck was tired and stained by bad luck at the moment when Britain desperately needed a winner. The new Commander in Chief Middle East was to be General Sir Harold Alexander, long marked for high command, handsome and distinguished, the perfect image of what a general should look like. To fill the vacant Eighth Army post, Churchill selected Strafer Gott. A warm and personable man who was without the slightest trace of fear, Gott had been at storm center of every fight in the desert since 1940.

Gott's record of generalship was hardly spotless, but he was without doubt the best-known and most-admired officer in the Eighth Army—and after the Gazala Gallop it suddenly became more important than ever for the men in the ranks to know and trust their commander. Ironically, the one general they had come to know above all others was the enemy's general.

The Rommel legend had grown to such epidemic pro-

The mobility of the desert armies is shown graphically in the photograph at left: a British Valentine tank stands abandoned in a desolate landscape cross-hatched with tracks. Above is the emblem of the Eighth Army.

IMPERIAL WAR MUSEUM, LONDON

portions in the Allied camp that Auchinleck had tried to check its spread with a warning to his officers. "There exists a real danger," he wrote, "that our friend Rommel is becoming a kind of magician or bogeyman to our troops, who are talking far too much about him. . . . Even if he were a superman, it would still be highly undesirable that our men should credit him with supernatural powers. . . . We must . . . not always keep harping on Rommel." The trouble was that the desert was an empty stage; the spectacular

These RAF pilots and their mascot were sketched by Anthony Gross at an Egyptian airfield in the late summer of 1942. In the background are their Hurricane fighter planes.

Prime Minister Churchill (right) and General Montgomery inspect the Eighth Army. It was Churchill's second visit to Egypt, a week after Montgomery took over.

BOTH: IMPERIAL WAR MUSEUM, LONDON

actions of a dramatic personality like the Desert Fox were bound to impress foe as well as friend.

The men of the Eighth Army knew only too well the speed and energy of Rommel's thrusts. From the stories of prisoners they also knew something of the hold he had over his men. They learned of his uncanny ability to be in the right place at the right time, of the charmed life he led fighting alongside the front-line troops, of the joking ways he had with the men in the ranks and the barracks-room language he used on officers who did not measure up. (After the war a motion picture called *The Desert Fox* was made, starring the English actor James Mason. When one of Rommel's officers was asked for his opinion of Mason's performance, he smiled and said, "Altogether too polite.") So the Rommel legend flourished, and gnawed at the Eighth Army's morale.

The day after Churchill made his command changes, a transport plane flying Strafer Gott to Cairo was shot down by a German fighter. Gott's death symbolized the end of an era. "Only Gott remained of the original men," correspondent Alan Moorehead reported, "and he stood out like a giant. . . . He was the last of the desert rats to go."

In Gott's place was appointed Lieutenant General Bernard Montgomery, a veteran of the Battle of France in

1940 and head of the forces stationed in the south of England. On August 15 Alexander and Montgomery took up the reins of command. With their arrival, as with Rommel's arrival eighteen months before, things began to happen.

Montgomery was fifty-five years old, small and wiry, with a long, thin nose and cold, pale blue eyes. He did not drink or smoke, and he disapproved of those who did; he had simple tastes and an "iron simplicity" of mind, with little interest in anything outside the problems of military command. Yet despite his austere personality, Montgomery had a remarkable flair for publicity. He deliberately set out to build himself up as the British champion; win, lose, or draw, the Eighth Army would know its commander and precisely what he expected of it.

BOTH: IMPERIAL WAR MUSEUM, LONDON

General Sir Harold Alexander had fought Germans in France and Japanese in Burma before taking over as commander in the Middle East.

Tirelessly, Montgomery poked about the army, sizing up its commanders, bringing in new men to replace those he found wanting (especially anyone who objected to his theories), learning the peculiarities of his troops. He found, for instance, that the New Zealanders had a casual attitude toward military discipline; when he remarked to their much-decorated general, Bernard Freyberg, that they never seemed to salute, Freyberg assured him, "Wave to them, sir, and they'll wave back." From then on Montgomery waved. Visiting the Australians, he adopted one of their wide-brimmed bush hats and decorated it with a selection of divisional badges; later he also adopted a tanker's beret. Before long a new spirit began to grow in the El Alamein lines—Monty was everywhere, Monty had taken hold, Monty was a go-getter. His stock went up further at the end of August, when he passed his first military test.

In his philosophy of command, Rommel drew a distinction between a bold attack and a gambling attack. Boldness in attack was always worth trying if it did not threaten the very existence of the army should it fail; a gamble was called for, he wrote, only when "defeat is merely a matter of time . . . and the only chance lies in an operation of great risk." By late August, 1942, he decided he must gamble.

Day by day the Panzerarmee Afrika was falling further and further behind in the battle of supply. Ships by the dozens, filled with troops from Britain and tanks from America, were steaming around Africa bound for Egypt. The inefficient Axis supply line, by contrast, sputtered along, barely able to keep up with daily needs and bringing nothing extra for battle needs. In August it brought Rommel 13,000 tons of supplies; the Eighth Army received 500,000 tons. Rommel would have to attack soon or the balance of strength tilting against him would make it impossible for him to attack at all.

On the last night of August the Afrika Korps swept through the southern end of the British line to open the Battle of Alam Halfa. It stumbled into unsuspected mine fields and was delayed. The next day, as Rommel attempted to turn in behind the British, his armor was pounded hard by artillery and bombers and became enmeshed in a cunning web of defenses. Grant tanks dug in on Alam Halfa Ridge did great execution.

By September 2 the Axis offensive was clearly stalled and in serious difficulty. What fuel was on hand had to be saved, for of three Italian gasoline tankers on their way to Tobruk one had been sunk and a second one damaged (it too was later sunk). As Rommel began to pull back, it seemed the moment for a vigorous counterattack. Montgomery, however, was content; he felt the Eighth Army was not yet in any condition to drive "headlong into the enemy." He had other plans for its use.

A British tanker gasses up his Crusader. Each Eighth Army armored division needed an average of 70,000 gallons of fuel a day.

Each pause between battles had brought a flow of new and better weapons to the desert, and this pause was no exception. The Panzerarmee managed to increase its supply of Mark III Specials fitted with the long 50-mm. guns. It also received some 30 new Mark IV Specials, each mounting a powerful long-barreled 75-mm. gun; they were probably the best tanks in the desert. There were 86 of the 88-mm. guns and 95 big antitank guns captured from the Russians that were almost as dangerous. Rommel had just over 100,000 men, half of them Italian. His main concern was how to supply them with the tools of war.

The Eighth Army, meanwhile, was receiving shipload after shipload of new tanks—American-built Shermans with 75-mm. guns. Tank for tank, the Sherman was perhaps a shade inferior to the Mark IV Special, but it had an overwhelming ten-to-one superiority in numbers. The 6-pounder antitank gun was now standard throughout the army, and self-propelled artillery—assault guns mounted on tank chassis—furnished additional firepower. By October, Montgomery's edge in manpower was two to one, and in heavily gunned tanks, more than five to one. His superiority in artillery, antitank guns, and air support was also substantial.

Such figures seemed almost to guarantee victory for the British but for the fact that the position at El Alamein was like nothing the two armies had seen before. In the past there had always been an open desert flank to invite a battle

of maneuver. At El Alamein both flanks were securely anchored—on the north by the sea and on the south by the forbidding Qattara Depression, a huge dished-out area 400 feet below sea level and full of salt marshes and quicksand. Into the 38 miles between these flanks Rommel had jammed 1,600 guns, 550 tanks, 100,000 men, and 500,000 land mines. Montgomery's edge in manpower and fire-power was not any too large for the kind of slugging match he expected to fight.

Operation Lightfoot, as the new British offensive was code-named, was carefully planned to take the best advantage of Eighth Army resources. The Australians, the New Zealanders, the Scottish Highlanders, were among the finest fighting troops in the world, and Montgomery built his assault around them. They were to breach the mine fields and overcome strong points, clearing a path for the armor. The tanks would then move up to form an iron shield to protect the infantry as it enveloped the remaining enemy positions, a process Montgomery called "crumbling." If Rommel counterattacked with tanks to save his infantry, the British armor would meet them defensively. Montgomery predicted the battle would last twelve days

IMPERIAL WAR MUSEUM, LONDON

The American-built Sherman tank (at left), like the Grant and the Stuart, was named for an American Civil War general. It had a crew of five and was armed with two machine guns and a powerful 75-mm. cannon. After the crushing British defeat at Gazala in June of 1942, President Roosevelt ordered 300 Shermans, slated for U.S. armored divisions, to be turned over to the Eighth Army; they played a vital role at El Alamein. The wooden gun and its scarecrow crew (right) was one of the many dummy weapons built before the battle to mislead Axis reconnaissance planes.

ELIOT ELISOFON, *Life* MAGAZINE © TIME, INC.

IMPERIAL WAR MUSEUM, LONDON

With a blaze of gun flashes and a thunderclap of noise, the British artillery opens the Battle of El Alamein. The 25-pounders making up the bulk of the Eighth Army's artillery fired an average of 102 rounds every day of the battle—over one million rounds in all.

and that it would result in complete defeat for the Panzerarmee Afrika.

Unable to fight his favorite battle of maneuver in such cramped quarters, the Desert Fox set out to make the cost of victory too high for the British to pay. The most awesome parts of the defenses were the belts of mine fields his men called the Devil's Gardens. They averaged some five miles in depth, and scattered through them were hundreds of strong points containing machine guns, mortars, and antitank guns. Behind the mine fields was a "gun line" of dug-in artillery and heavy antitank guns. Nearby, tanks were poised to move toward any breakthrough.

Most of the mines in the Devil's Gardens were the antitank type, rigged to go off under the weight of a vehicle (or a running man); they would destroy any truck that ran over them and cripple tanks by blowing off their tracks. Thickly sown among these large mines were thousands of small S-mines, deadly to infantry. If stepped on, a charge shot them two or three feet in the air, where they exploded. Many mines were cunningly boobytrapped so that if they were moved they set off other mines nearby. Stretched just above the ground were trip wires attached to the firing pins of 250-pound aircraft bombs. All these deadly devices were easy to plant and conceal in the desert's sandy surface.

The Desert Fox was not on hand to supervise the defenses he had planned. A year and a half of hard campaigning had left him seriously ill, and in September he was recalled to Germany for medical treatment. General Georg Stumme was sent from the Russian front to replace him. On his way home Rommel saw both Mussolini and Hitler and complained bitterly about the supply crisis, but nothing was done. "It is sometimes a misfortune to enjoy a certain military reputation," he wrote in exasperation. "One knows one's own limits but others expect miracles."

Montgomery scheduled Operation Lightfoot to begin at night, in the light of a full moon. Four infantry divisions were to crack open the Axis line near its northern end. With the foot soldiers would go parties of sappers to search out mines, remove them, and mark safe corridors for the following armor. Nearly 900 pieces of heavy artillery would support the attack, and the RAF guaranteed control of the air. Elaborate camouflage and fleets of dummy vehicles concealed the point of attack.

Zero hour for the Battle of El Alamein was set for 9:40 on the night of October 23, 1942. At that moment, with one tremendous roar, 882 field guns loosed a rain of high explosives on the Panzerarmee. The sweating gunners rammed in shell after shell, and the gun barrels glowed with heat. Howard Kippenberger, commander of a New Zealand brigade, recalled how "the maddening incessant clamour of the guns became deafening"; for some slight shelter against the "uproar and the concussion" he and his staff crouched behind a truck. In the moonlight the infantry could be seen moving forward at a walk, holding their rifles with fixed bayonets at the ready. Sappers advanced with them, probing for mines with bayonets and

OVERLEAF: *Terence Cuneo's painting commemorates the work of the sappers of the Royal Engineers at El Alamein. Clearing corridors through the Axis mine fields at night and under fire was slow and nerve-racking, and the casualties were severe. Mines were located by probing with bayonets or by the electric mine-detectors shown here; a "pinging" was heard in the earphones as the mine detector passed over metal. The man crouching at center puts a metal cone over each mine; other sappers later removed the mines. The white tape marks the edge of the cleared corridor.*

BY COURTESY OF THE ROYAL ENGINEERS CORPS COMMITTEE

electric mine-detectors. The waiting, dew-covered tanks glistened blackly in the dazzling gun flashes. Slowly there spread over the battlefield a thick, choking cloud of dust.

As the infantrymen plodded forward they watched closely for the stalklike prongs that marked S-mines. Here and there men were hit and fell writhing in the sand. The staccato bursts of German machine guns and the skirling of the Scottish Highlanders' bagpipes could be heard above the thunder of the barrage. In the thickening dust, attackers and defenders tangled blindly in vicious fire-fights.

BOTH: IMPERIAL WAR MUSEUM, LONDON

Australian infantrymen support a wounded German they captured.

Meanwhile, amidst the bullets and the shells, the sappers went about their exacting tasks. With detectors or bayonets they located mines, gingerly felt around them for trip wires and other booby traps, lifted them out and removed their detonators, and stacked them off to the side. White tapes and colored lights were put up to mark the cleared corridors. As they worked, masses of tanks and trucks and guns began to crawl forward. In the jam many of the sappers' markers were knocked down, and vehicles blundered onto uncleared mines. By dawn the infantry had reached most of its objectives, but the armor was still enmeshed in the Devil's Gardens.

In the Axis headquarters all was confusion. The massive bombardment had torn up the Panzerarmee's communications links, and the forward posts could not get their information back to the high command. General Stumme set out to see for himself what was happening. Nearing the front, his car was caught by a blast of fire from Australian infantrymen. Stumme's aide was killed, and just as the general started to get out to seek cover, the driver whirled the car around to escape. As Stumme clung desperately to the side of the speeding car he suffered a heart attack and tumbled dead to the ground. General Ritter von Thoma of the Afrika Korps took over command of the army. In Germany, Rommel was alerted to the British attack; that evening Hitler himself telephoned to ask him to return to North Africa.

Montgomery's brisk order for the first day of battle called for the armor to fight on through the mine fields, regardless of its losses. By dusk, the 1st Armored Division had done so, beating off counterattacks by the Afrika Korps. But that night, when the 10th Armored Division tried to carry out Montgomery's orders, it ran into an inferno of resistance.

As the division's 250 tanks and their supporting vehicles churned through the foot-deep dust in the narrow mine-

Under the cover of a smoke screen, Australians storm an enemy strong point. The 9th Australian Division suffered nearly 3,000 casualties at El Alamein, the greatest loss of all Eighth Army divisions.

field corridors, German planes lit the battlefield as brightly as day with parachute flares and dropped bombs into the tightly packed mass of transport. Ammunition and gasoline trucks blazed in one "enormous crackling furnace which lit the desert up for a radius of two miles," in the words of an eyewitness. The burning trucks became aiming points for the enemy artillery. Taking heavy losses, 10th Armored pressed on, and by the morning of October 25, some of its units had linked up with 1st Armored.

Montgomery finally had his armored shield for the in-

A column of Scottish Highlanders, led by their bagpiper (center), moves through a cleared mine-field corridor toward the front lines during the El Alamein fighting. The wire fence marks the edge of the cor-

IMPERIAL WAR MUSEUM, LONDON

ridor. At left, soldiers pause to "brew up"; at the right is a Bren carrier, a fast-moving tracked vehicle for carrying troops. War artist Jack Chaddock painted this water color from sketches he made on the battlefield.

fantry bridgehead, but no true breakthrough had been made. Behind the mine fields the enemy's gun line was intact, and with daylight it began taking a heavy toll of the British armor. A tank officer helplessly watched the Grants of his regiment "go up in sheets of flame one by one, just as if someone had lit the candles on a birthday cake," under the fire of concealed 88's.

On its third day the Battle of El Alamein was approaching stalemate. The Eighth Army had broken into the enemy's position but could get no farther; the enemy was equally frustrated when he tried to counterattack. One of Montgomery's corps commanders recalled that on October 26 "we were within an ace of losing our grip on the battle." Casualties among the attacking infantry and the sappers had been particularly heavy—the total of dead, wounded, and missing was already more than 6,100—and exhaustion was becoming a problem. Some 300 British tanks had been knocked out, but this was no great worry—Montgomery had 800 more on call.

To retain the initiative, Montgomery decided to shift the weight of his attack to the extreme northern end of the line, near the coast road, where the Australians had seized some key ground. The infantry and armored units that had borne the brunt of the battle so far would be pulled back to rest and refit.

Rommel, who had now arrived to take over command, also made a key decision that day. The breaching of the Devil's Gardens had removed his best chance for a "negative victory"—a stalemated battle. From now on, he thought, the Panzerarmee Afrika would be steadily ground down by superior weight. Characteristically, he chose to gamble with an armored counterattack before this weight became crushing.

That night a 300-man British detachment, most of them tough London Cockneys, seized an advance post near an objective code-named Snipe. Unknown to them, they were close by the line of advance Rommel's armor was to follow in its counterattack the next day. At first light on October 27 the Snipe detachment discovered it was in a hot spot.

Through the morning the Cockneys pitted their nineteen antitank guns against relays of German and Italian

Armored and infantry units of both armies are positioned here as they began the battle. Montgomery's three main thrusts are illustrated by arrows: breaching the mine fields, the dogfight in the north, the breakthrough.

THE BATTLE OF EL ALAMEIN
October 23—November 4, 1942
Axis Infantry
British Infantry
Axis Mine Fields
Phases of the battle
Coast Road
15th PANZER
Gun Line
LITTORIO
21st PANZER
ARIETE
9th AUSTRALIAN
51st HIGHLAND
NEW ZEALAND
1st SOUTH AFRICAN
2nd BRIGADE
8th BRIGADE
24th BRIGADE
9th BRIGADE
El Alamein
4th INDIAN
50th BRITISH
44th BRITISH
4th BRIGADE
22nd BRIGADE
QATTARA DEPRESSION

tanks sent to dispose of them. The armor came off a poor second. Before long more than a dozen tanks were burning or disabled. A big Mark IV Special rumbled to within 30 yards of the post before a shot from one of the 6-pounders set it ablaze.

Shortly after noon a determined assault by Italian tanks came perilously close to overrunning the position. Only one gun was sited to meet the attack, and it was soon out of ammunition. As three tanks closed in, a jeep carrying ammunition raced up to the silent gun, was hit, and burst into flames. The ammunition was saved, however, and gunner Charles Caliston calmly aimed and fired three times, killing all three tanks. Just as calmly, he then brewed up a mug of tea on the hood of the burning jeep.

The Snipe action reached a climax in late afternoon when the 21st Panzer Division passed by in its counterattack on the British bridgehead. Tank after tank was jolted by solid shot that glowed red as it bored through armor. Some twenty tanks and self-propelled guns were knocked out, disrupting the entire attack. That night the survivors of Snipe withdrew with their one serviceable gun. They had destroyed 37 enemy tanks and mobile guns and damaged another 15 to 20.

Savagely, Montgomery pressed the Australians' attack

A British aid station at El Alamein, sketched by Anthony Gross. The overflow of wounded men finds shelter under a makeshift tent. In the background is an ambulance.

BOTH: IMPERIAL WAR MUSEUM, LONDON

After a week of severe fighting, Rommel wrote his wife: "The enemy, with his superior strength, is slowly levering us out of our position." Here, British infantry take shelter from a shellburst behind a disabled Panzer Mark III.

in the north, and just as savagely the Germans resisted it. Some of Rommel's best formations, including the veteran 90th Light Division, had to be thrown into the fight. Gains were measured in yards, and the intensity of the artillery fire and the bombing surpassed anything seen before in the desert. "The situation continues very grave," Rommel wrote his wife on October 29. "By the time this letter arrives, it will no doubt have been decided whether we can hold on or not. I haven't much hope left." Two gasoline tankers he had been counting on had just been sunk at Tobruk by RAF bombers. He had used precious fuel to mass his armor and his last reserves in the north to hold Montgomery's attack, and there was very little left for further maneuvering.

Frustrated in this second attempt at a breakthrough, Montgomery coolly switched the weight of his attack once more. He believed, he told London, that Rommel "is now ripe for a real hard blow which may topple him off his perch." General Freyberg's New Zealand Division was reinforced by English and Scottish brigades to lead the way; the refitted 1st and 10th armored divisions would exploit the advance. The objective of the new assault, set for the early hours of November 2, was the final Axis gun line beyond the mine fields.

On this night, as they had on the first night of battle, the infantry and the sappers fought their way to their ob-

Something of the spirit of El Alamein's climax is captured in this water color by Alex Ingram. Sherman tanks spurt into the clear beyond the mine-filled Devil's Gardens. Overhead is the Desert Air Force. The 530 British and American planes overwhelmed the Luftwaffe and played havoc with Rommel's army and its supply line.

jectives. The artillery "storm" supporting them consumed 15,000 shells. Then came the armor, spearheaded by the 123 tanks of the 9th Armored Brigade. Its commander, Brigadier John Currie, had been told that he must break the gun line and that the army commander was willing to accept 100 per cent casualties to do it.

At first light, Currie's 9th Armored Brigade charged, as the famous Light Brigade had charged at Balaklava in the Crimean War almost a century before—with the same terrible result. Twenty or so well-sited 88's opened up with

IMPERIAL WAR MUSEUM, LONDON

fearful effect. "The whole world seemed to blow up at once," remembered one of Currie's officers. The shriek of 88-mm. high-velocity shells, and the harsh clang as they struck the tanks, dominated all other sounds. The armor overran and destroyed some 35 smaller guns, but it could not reach the 88's. As the sun rose it tinted blood-red the pillars of oily smoke from knocked-out tanks. Derelict Shermans and Grants and Crusaders were scattered thickly in every direction; one had been hit so hard that it was pitched over on its side. All told, Currie lost 103 of his tanks, a casualty rate of nearly 85 per cent. The Axis gun line was bent but not broken.

Throughout the rest of the day a fierce tank battle raged

A German 88-mm. gun, blackened by fire, and its smashed half-track hauler are inspected by the El Alamein victors. The battle cost Rommel 50 of his deadly 88's.

IMPERIAL WAR MUSEUM, LONDON—HUBERT FREETH

General von Thoma of the Afrika Korps, sketched after his capture.

IMPERIAL WAR MUSEUM, LONDON

as Rommel strove to contain the two armored divisions threatening his last line of defense. Losses were heavy on both sides, but they were losses that Montgomery could afford and Rommel could not. The killing match was almost over.

On November 3 the Desert Fox began to withdraw his surviving infantry behind one of his always dangerous screens of armor and antitank guns. It was a day of frustration for the Eighth Army. Casualties in men and equipment had been high, and in the billowing dust and smoke it seemed that the carnage would never end. Late in the afternoon, however, Montgomery received an unexpected helping hand from Adolf Hitler. The Führer ordered Rommel to "stand fast, yield not a yard of ground, and throw every gun and every man into the battle." There must be "no other road than that to victory or death," he warned his commander in North Africa.

So Rommel stood fast and fought another day and lost his last chance for an orderly retreat. On November 4 victory came swiftly; as Montgomery had predicted, it was the twelfth day of battle. Most of the Italian infantry was without trucks and had to surrender. "The tanks came plunging through, hundreds of tanks lunging to the west through the gap . . . and wheeling north for the kill," wrote the historian of the Indian Division. The remnants of the Afrika Korps withdrew along the coast road; any units without transport had to escape on foot or surrender. Some 30,000 men gave themselves up. In a last effort to stem the tide rushing over him, Afrika Korps' General von Thoma attacked in his command tank, escaped as it went up in flames, and then stood quietly on the smoking battlefield, waiting to be taken.

Ahead of the Eighth Army, wrote an eyewitness, "stretched nothing but death and destruction to the very horizon. Shattered trucks, burnt and contorted tanks, blackened and tangled heaps of wreckage not to be recognized; they scattered the landscape as thickly as stars in the sky. . . . In dugouts, pits, and trenches the dead lay tangled and piled. . . . These were details of the scene repeated again and again in every corner of the desert landscape: a great rubbish heap of metal and human flesh. So the victors sat, gazing across the gigantic desolation. . . ."

To herald the long-awaited desert victory, Winston Churchill ordered the church bells to peal out from one end of Britain to the other. El Alamein, he wrote, marked "the turning of the Hinge of Fate."

VI OPERATION TORCH

NATIONAL MARITIME MUSEUM, GREENWICH

Less than 48 hours before Montgomery's thundering guns opened the Battle of El Alamein, three British commandos and five United States Army officers landed on a dark and deserted beach on the coast of French Algeria, some 2,500 miles to the west. Lying offshore in the Mediterranean was the British submarine *Seraph*, which had brought them there. As they quickly hid their canoes in a grove of trees behind the beach, American diplomat Robert Murphy ap-

British artist Richard Eurich depicted camouflaged supply ships and troop transports (left foreground) in a vast Operation Torch convoy.

SIGNAL CORPS—U.S. ARMY

General Mark W. Clark was forty-six when he became Eisenhower's deputy commander for Operation Torch. He led U.S. forces during the Italian campaign later in the war.

peared out of the darkness to greet them. "Welcome to North Africa," Murphy whispered. Major General Mark W. Clark, still panting from his exertions, replied simply but with feeling, "I'm damn glad we made it." They raked the sand smooth over their tracks and hurried to a house on a bluff overlooking the beach.

Shortly after dawn on October 22 another group of men arrived by car from the capital city of Algiers, 75 miles away. After an exchange of greetings, the newcomers, carrying suitcases, marched into bedrooms and soon emerged wearing uniforms of the French armed forces. After a hurried breakfast, everyone sat down to a long round of discussions, arguments, and exchanges of military information.

That afternoon the owner of the house received a telephone call and shouted excitedly that the police were approaching. Since the Americans were violating the rights of a neutral nation, and the French officers were committing treason, pandemonium broke loose. Some of the Frenchmen ran for their cars after scrambling back into civilian clothes with a speed, General Clark noted, that "I have seen exceeded only by professional quick-change artists." Others jumped out of windows and dashed into the woods. Clark and his aides scurried through a trap door into a dusty wine cellar.

When the police burst in a few minutes later, they found diplomat Murphy and three companions around a table littered with wine bottles, playing poker. The sudden activity at the secluded house, Murphy explained innocently, was only "a little party." He was sure, he added, that the police would not embarrass him further by disturbing the "ladies" upstairs. After poking about suspiciously, the police left.

With the talks so abruptly ended, Clark decided to leave as soon as it was dark. The *Seraph*, which had submerged during the day, surfaced and moved to within 100 yards of the shore. But the wind had risen and breakers were crashing across the beach. When the canoes were put into the water, they immediately capsized. Stripped to their shorts, Clark and his men tried again and again to launch the frail craft; in the confusion the general's pants and $2,000 in gold, brought along "for possible use in buying our way out of a jam," went to the bottom. At last, with the help of Murphy and his staff, all four canoes made it safely through the pounding surf. As dawn was breaking, the *Seraph* snatched up the bedraggled party, submerged, and headed for Gibraltar.

Clark's secret mission, full of boldness, derring-do, and

confusion, was perfectly typical of Operation Torch. The Torch plan called for the United States, heavily supported by her British ally, to invade the French North African possessions of Morocco and Algeria. In victory or defeat, Torch was sure to be spectacular. An amphibious assault from the sea is one of war's most complex operations, and the Americans were making not one but three landings. No one knew whether the troops would be greeted with bouquets or bullets; in fact, it was entirely possible that Torch would tip the balance against the Allies rather than for them.

After the fall of France in 1940, German troops had occupied only half the country and none of France's African territories. In return, the government of Marshal Henri Pétain at Vichy in southern France cooperated with the Nazis. Pétain, France's great hero of World War I, required all ranking officers of the French armed forces to honor the armistice that had ended the fighting and to swear a personal oath of loyalty to him.

UPI

American diplomat Robert W. Murphy, assigned to the neutral Vichy government ruling France, worked in North Africa two years to win friends for the Allied cause.

This left the officers in North Africa in a painful quandary. Military honor—which meant a great deal to a French officer—clearly required them to obey Marshal Pétain's orders to oppose an Allied attack. But it was equally clear to most of them that Nazi Germany, not the Allies, was France's mortal enemy. Their dilemma was how to uphold their honor and still serve the best interests of their country.

To further tangle an already tangled situation, many of these officers bore a bitter grudge against their onetime ally Great Britain. In part this was because Britain supported French general Charles de Gaulle, who had denounced the armistice and had rallied Free French forces—thus implying that any general or admiral loyal to Marshal Pétain was a traitor. But most of all, their hatred dated from July 3, 1940, when the Royal Navy attacked and severely crippled a French fleet at Oran in Algeria to prevent it from falling into German hands. Torch would have to be an all-American operation—or at least look like one.

The driving force behind Torch came from Prime Minister Churchill and President Roosevelt. Churchill had long and vigorously supported a Mediterranean grand strategy, while Roosevelt was insistent that American forces join the fight against Hitler in 1942. When it became clear that the Allies were not yet strong enough to dare a frontal attack on the Nazis across the English Channel, the two leaders settled on northwest Africa as the target. Their decision

BROWN BROTHERS

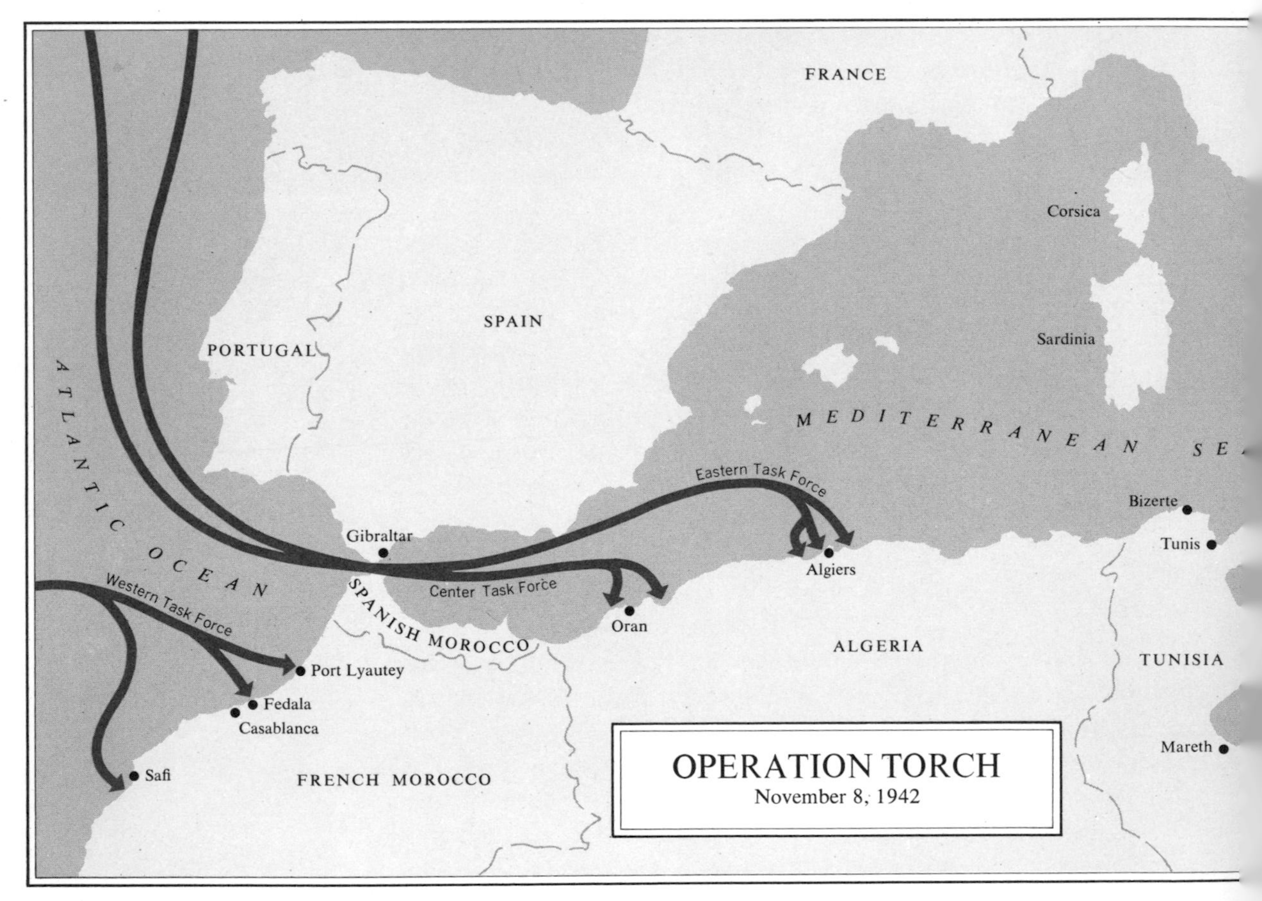

was made on July 25, 1942, as Auchinleck fought Rommel to a standstill at El Alamein. "Now we are on our way shoulder to shoulder," Roosevelt wrote to Churchill.

Not only would Torch deny a large part of the North African coast to the Axis, but successful landings and a rapid advance into Tunisia would trap Rommel in the Western Desert. Control of the Mediterranean sea lanes would be in Allied hands, and the entire southern flank of Europe—"the soft underbelly," as Churchill liked to call it—would be uncovered.

Left: Prime Minister Churchill (in naval cap) and President Roosevelt meeting in Washington. Roosevelt overruled his military advisers in approving the Torch plan. The routes of Torch task forces are shown below. The Oran and Algiers convoys sailed from England, the Casablanca convoy from ports in the United States.

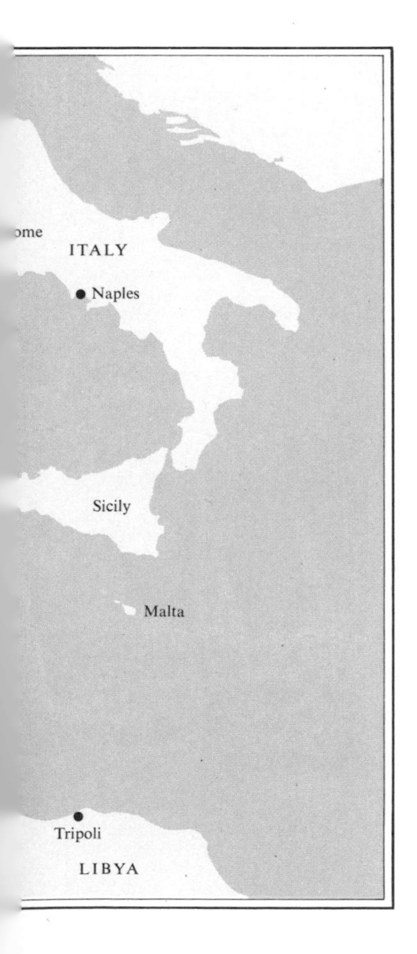

Set against these advantages was the chance that France would fight, perhaps routing the invaders or even going over entirely to the Axis camp. A stronger possibility was that Hitler would funnel an army into Tunisia from Sicily (only 90 miles away) and gain passage through neutral Spain for a second army to seize the Strait of Gibraltar. If this happened, it would be the Torch forces that would be trapped.

Despite all these unpleasant ifs, the war situation in the summer of 1942 demanded Allied action of the boldest kind. The road to victory seemed to stretch ahead endlessly, and if Torch would provide a short cut, Roosevelt and Churchill were willing to gamble on it. But it would have to be done soon. There were hints that the Germans planned to occupy French North Africa. After November, bad weather would prevent any amphibious operations until spring—probably too late. The Torch planning headquarters in London, under the command of Lieutenant General Dwight D. Eisenhower, set to work at a furious pace.

After much argument and juggling of forces, it was decided to make three simultaneous landings. Two convoys would sail from England, slip through the Strait of Gibraltar into the Mediterranean, and land at Oran and Algiers in Algeria. To guard against an enemy seizure of the strait, a third convoy would sail directly from the United States to occupy Casablanca, on the Atlantic coast of French Morocco. This would open an emergency life line to the Torch forces in the Mediterranean over the railroad connecting Casablanca and Oran. The assault troops at all three points would be American, followed ashore by the British—"with plenty of American flags," Churchill remarked. Until landing fields could be captured, air cover would be provided by aircraft carriers. The target date (D-day) was set for November 8, 1942.

While Eisenhower and his commanders dealt with the

million and one military details of the operation, Robert Murphy, the chief American diplomat assigned to North Africa, was trying to smooth the way for the invading troops. Carefully sounding out French officers, he assembled an underground network of those friendly to the Allied cause. Their role would be to take over key strong points on D-day. The secret mission of General Clark, Eisenhower's second in command, was a part of this cloak-and-dagger plot.

The plotters needed to find someone besides Marshal Pétain that the French armed forces would rally to, someone who would quickly come to terms with the American invaders and get the 120,000-man French army in North Africa into the battle against the Axis. They chose General Henri Giraud, who had escaped from a German prison camp and had strong anti-Nazi opinions.

Another figure to be reckoned with was Admiral Jean Darlan, head of the French Navy. Darlan was a shifty character with an unsavory reputation for cooperating with the Nazis, but he would probably join whichever side seemed the strongest. If the Allies won him over, he would bring the French fleet along with him. Because so many French generals and admirals opposed him, General de Gaulle was given no role in Operation Torch.

In late October the 650 ships involved in Torch began steaming from various ports toward North Africa. Very few of the thousands of soldiers, sailors, and airmen had any combat experience, and many of them were short of training as well. The last amphibious operation the United States Army had undertaken was in the Spanish-American War in 1898. But the risks had to be taken. "There are times in history when we cannot afford to wait for the final polish," wrote British admiral Sir Andrew Cunningham, naval commander of Torch, and in Cunningham's opinion this was one such time.

On November 5 General Eisenhower arrived at his operational headquarters at Gibraltar. He and his staff were greeted with the news of Montgomery's victory at El Alamein, and that night they watched the darkened ships of the Oran and Algiers convoys glide through the narrow Strait of Gibraltar. Axis agents in neutral Spanish territory could not help but see the ships too, but it was assumed that they were headed for Malta or Egypt. The German and Italian high commands laid plans to ambush them off Sicily.

By the early morning hours of November 8, the Center

NATIONAL ARCHIVES

Life-jacketed American infantrymen packed aboard a troop transport off Oran were photographed during a lifeboat drill. The Royal Navy warships protecting the Oran convoy included a battleship, a heavy aircraft carrier, two light carriers, and thirteen destroyers.

Task Force was in position off Oran. At 3 A.M. the *Hartland* and the *Walney*, onetime U.S. Coast Guard cutters turned over to the British, made a dash for the harbor to try to seize ships and port installations before the French could sabotage them. They missed the narrow entrance in the darkness; as the cutters maneuvered for another try, searchlights flicked on along the shore.

With the *Walney* leading the way, the cutters charged again, smashing through two floating booms strung across the harbor mouth to keep out enemy submarines. By now the defenders were fully alert. Searchlights held the two ships fast in their brilliant grip, and guns of all kinds poured out a murderous storm of fire at them.

Nearing the spot where she was to land her assault forces, the *Walney* came under the point-blank fire of the guns of a pair of French destroyers. Literally torn to pieces, her decks piled high with dead and dying, the *Walney* lost all power, burst into flames, and blew up. The *Hartland* fared little better. Her gun crews were wiped out to a man, and a French destroyer pumped shell after shell into her at a range of 100 feet. The survivors abandoned ship as the burning cutter drifted aimlessly with the tide.

Despite this disastrous beginning, the Oran operation went like clockwork. The 39,000 assault troops streamed ashore on beaches some twenty miles east and west of the city. The French were surprised, but their opposition was sharp despite the abundance of American flags carried by the invaders. Fighting continued that day and the next as the Americans consolidated their beachheads and closed in on Oran. On the morning of November 10 the city surrendered.

At Algiers, meanwhile, the action had been more polit-

IMPERIAL WAR MUSEUM, LONDON

ical than military. At three landing beaches flanking the city the British and American troops came ashore against scarcely any opposition at all. As the landing forces formed up and began moving on Algiers itself, the city was in an advanced state of confusion. Murphy's underground plotters had gone into action. Bands of young rebels armed with a rag-tag of weapons seized the radio station, the central telephone switchboard, police stations, and even some military headquarters. By two o'clock on D-day morning, as scheduled, the plotters were ready to hand Algiers over to the Americans without a drop of blood being shed. But no Americans appeared. They were ten or fifteen miles away. What the underground had not been told, because of the need for secrecy, was that the landings would take

Reinforcements pour ashore from landing craft at a beach near Algiers. To make certain the French knew the identity of the invaders, a man at left carries a large American flag. The troops also wore American-flag armbands. What little opposition there was at Algiers came mainly from coastal defense guns firing at the ships offshore.

place on beaches well to the east and west of the city.

With infinite pains, one observer noted, Robert Murphy "had assembled a nicely filled apple cart"; now the American diplomat was desperately trying to keep it from being kicked over. As the rebels ranged the city, Murphy hurried to the home of the French North African army commander, General Alphonse Juin. General Juin was in sympathy with the Allies, but he could not declare a ceasefire without the approval of his superior, Admiral Darlan, who had unexpectedly appeared in Algiers. Juin telephoned Darlan and asked him to join them right away.

It was not yet 2 A.M. when Darlan arrived. As Murphy told him of Operation Torch, Darlan exploded in wrath at what he called an unprovoked attack. While the short, stocky admiral angrily paced back and forth, the tall American diplomat paced alongside him, trying to match his steps to the short strides of the Frenchman and pleading with him to "strike an effective blow now for the liberation of France" by declaring a ceasefire. But Darlan had decided on a waiting game, to see if the Americans were really arriving in the strength that Murphy claimed. With the excuse that he would have to get in touch with Marshal Pétain, the admiral began to stall.

At dawn on D-day the Vichy radio began to broadcast over and over Marshal Pétain's statement—"We are attacked. We shall defend ourselves. That is the order I am giving." Vichy police and military units set about reclaiming the key points in Algiers and hauling the rebels away to jail. Police arrived at General Juin's home, overpowered the rebels that surrounded it, and put Murphy under arrest.

After a final dizzy whirl, the situation in Algiers was stabilized. One of the rebels managed to reach General Charles Ryder, commander of the American landing forces, and pleaded with him to abandon the methodical, carefully planned encirclement of the city. Algiers was Ryder's for the taking, the Frenchman said—"but by noon it will be too late." Ryder ordered a swift, direct advance, and late that afternoon a local ceasefire was arranged. At dusk on November 8 Algiers was in Allied hands.

Admiral Darlan, however, was not ready to abandon his slippery game just yet. He refused to order an armistice for all French North Africa, nor would he order French forces in Tunisia to prevent German troops from landing there. His hand was strengthened when General Giraud, the "big name" Murphy had been counting on, arrived the next day in Algiers. It turned out that Giraud had no sup-

U.S. ARMY

General Eisenhower makes a forceful point in a conversation with Admiral Darlan. The admiral was widely accused of being a Nazi collaborator; Eisenhower disliked him and dealt with him only to save Allied and French lives. Churchill felt the same. If Darlan would bring the French fleet over to the Allies, he said, "much as I hate him, I would cheerfully crawl on my hands and knees for a mile. . . ."

port at all, and he was ignored by everyone but the Americans. Only Darlan seemed to have the power of decision, and Darlan was going to wait a bit longer to see which way to jump. As a result, several hundred Americans and Frenchmen died unnecessarily at Oran and Casablanca.

The assault on Casablanca was the biggest gamble of all, for the Atlantic coastal waters were seldom calm that late in the year. As the Western Task Force approached the Moroccan coast, weather forecasters in Washington and London predicted a storm and a fifteen-foot surf on November 8, too high for landing craft. But the task force's own weatherman insisted that the storm would pass. The advice of the man on the spot was taken, and by the early hours of D-day, as the ships took position off Casablanca, the Atlantic was as calm as a millpond. The assault troops waited nervously, with only a few lights and the smell of charcoal smoke indicating that land was nearby. "Africa was never so dark and mysterious to ancient sea rovers as she seemed that night to these seventy thousand young men," wrote an eyewitness, historian Samuel Eliot Morison.

The Casablanca landings, like those at Oran and Algiers, were made at beaches flanking the city. The main force, landing at a fishing village called Fedala, fifteen miles north of Casablanca, met little resistance. Its chief troubles came from batteries of coastal defense guns firing at the ships offshore, but before long, American cruisers and destroyers had silenced them. The light cruiser *Brooklyn*, for example, rained 757 shells from her 6-inch guns on one coastal battery in a little more than an hour.

At Safi, well to the south of Casablanca, the landing operation was as smooth as silk. It was decided to attack the port head-on, the old destroyers *Bernadou* and *Cole* leading the way with loads of specially trained assault troops. Their sudden arrival out of the darkness triggered a blast of gunfire from the defenders, but the destroyers returned the fire with such accuracy that they all but silenced the entire harbor defense system. Before the day was far along, Safi was firmly under control, Sherman tanks were put ashore on the wharves, and the army could count only 29 casualties in the landing.

The northernmost landing at Port Lyautey, by contrast, was the most fiercely contested of any in Operation Torch. Landing operations got into a fearful tangle, with landing craft coming ashore late, at the wrong places, and then be-

German reaction to the Torch landings was swift, with the Luftwaffe striking at the ships off Algiers on the afternoon of D-day. This picture, taken during another German bombing raid the next night, shows tracer shells from the Allied ships' guns lacing the sky.

IMPERIAL WAR MUSEUM, LONDON

ing wrecked as they grounded. The defenses were well handled, and reinforcements were close by. For a time the invaders were in a critical situation, but finally they began to gain the upper hand. Carrier planes helped break up a counterattack by French tanks, and the battleship *Texas* reached seven miles inland with its main battery of 14-inch guns to shatter a truck convoy full of reinforcements. Yet it took four days of hard fighting and cost close to 400 American casualties before Port Lyautey's stubborn defenders were overwhelmed.

While the three landing forces flanking the city were consolidating their beachheads on D-day, a savage naval battle was raging off Casablanca itself. This was a tragic and unnecessary action, the bitter fruit of Admiral Darlan's little game; hearing nothing to the contrary from Darlan, Admiral François Michelier at Casablanca obeyed Pétain's orders to fight.

Michelier had eleven submarines, nine destroyers, and a light cruiser ready for sea, backed up by several batteries of coast-defense guns and the unfinished battleship *Jean Bart*, unable to sail but with her 15-inch guns operational. To guard against any French naval action, and to screen the landing operations at nearby Fedala, American admiral Kent Hewitt had the new battleship *Massachusetts*, one light and three heavy cruisers, and more than a dozen destroyers, plus planes from the fleet carrier *Ranger* and a small escort carrier.

The problem of the *Jean Bart* was quickly solved. The French battleship opened fire on the *Massachusetts* at 7 A.M., narrowly missing the big battlewagon, which replied immediately. Within twenty minutes, five of her massive 16-inch shells had hit the *Jean Bart*, one of them putting the main battery out of action. The American warships had less luck silencing the pesky shore batteries.

An hour later, Admiral Michelier ordered seven of his destroyers and the light cruiser *Primauguet* to strike out after the troop transports and landing craft off Fedala. A black-robed priest stood on the breakwater, blessing the doomed ships as they steamed past. Admiral Hewitt's warships converged to meet them. For an hour and a half the outgunned French made skillful use of smoke screens and maneuvered radically to avoid the hail of shells splashing around them.

Their good luck could not last forever. A salvo from the *Massachusetts* and one from the heavy cruiser *Tuscaloosa* hit a French destroyer at the same time and blew her to pieces.

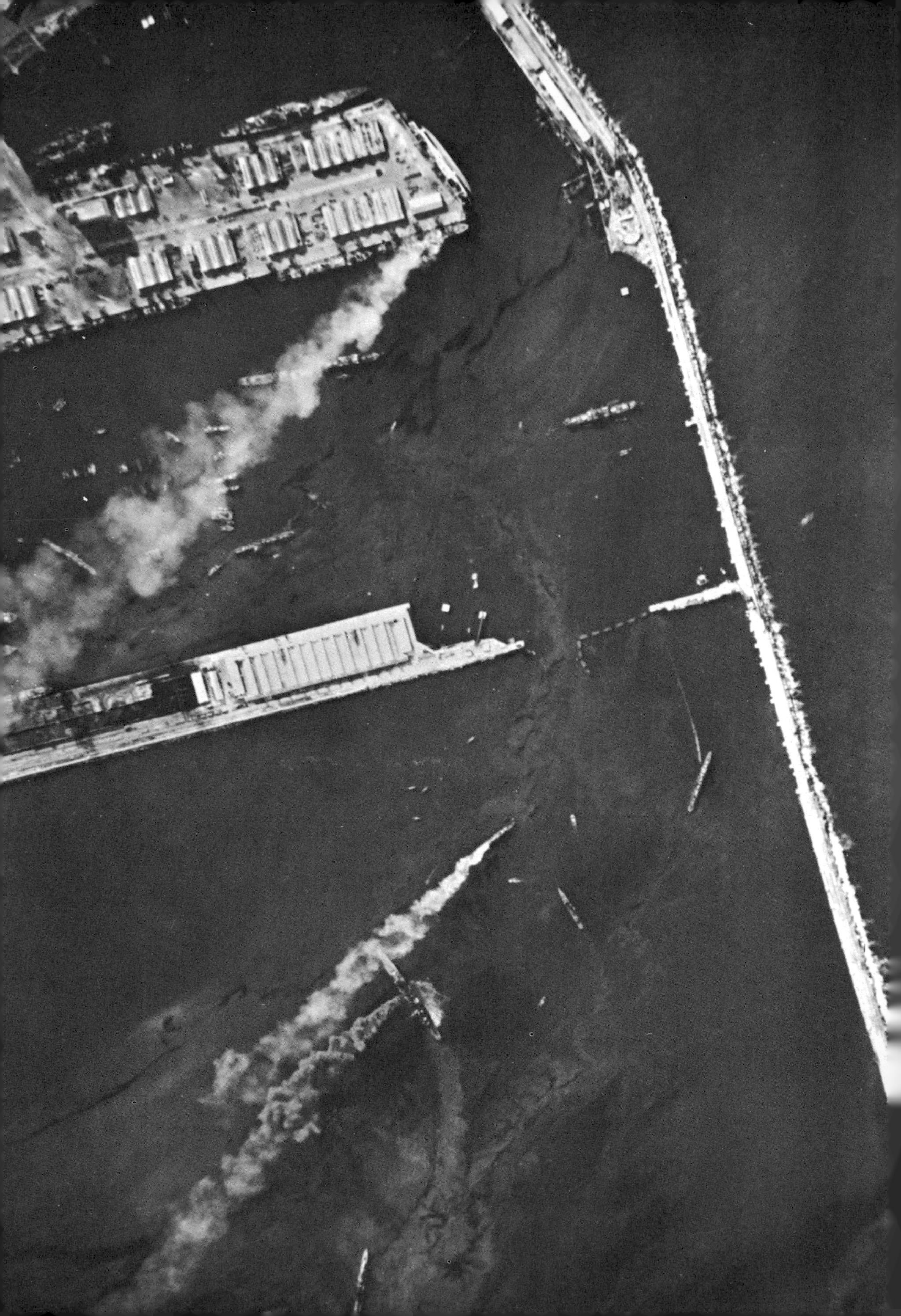

The light cruiser *Brooklyn* sent another destroyer to the bottom, and along with the heavy cruiser *Augusta*, mangled the *Primauguet*, killing two thirds of her crew. Fighter planes from the *Ranger* caused heavy casualties by strafing the French ships. By noon the gallant sortie of Michelier's squadron was over. Two of his ships were sunk, a third was dead in the water, abandoned and burning, and four other cripples had limped back to Casablanca and beached themselves in the harbor. All of the eighteen or so torpedoes fired by French submarines in the engagement missed; the American force took five minor hits by naval or shore guns and lost one landing craft.

On November 10 General Mark Clark confronted Admiral Darlan in Algiers. Towering menacingly over the little admiral, Clark told him bluntly that he had the choice of ordering a ceasefire throughout North Africa or going to prison—and he had 30 minutes to make up his mind. Darlan gave the necessary orders, and the next day the fighting at Casablanca ended.

The ceasefire marked the end of Operation Torch. If it created more political problems than it solved, as a military operation it was a brilliant success—a fact the enemy realized only too well. On D-day, as news poured in of the landings at Casablanca, Oran, and Algiers, a German staff officer stationed in Morocco exclaimed to a French official: "This is the greatest setback to German arms since 1918. The Americans will take Rommel in the rear, and we shall be expelled from Africa." As he said it, the Frenchman noted, tears rolled down his cheeks.

IMPERIAL WAR MUSEUM, LONDON—H. H. MCWILLIAMS

The aerial view at left is Casablanca's harbor after the naval battle of November 8. The battleship Jean Bart *is at top, alongside the large pier. At lower center, trailing smoke, is the light cruiser* Primauguet. *The drawing looks across the large pier toward the* Jean Bart*'s superstructure.*

VII

MASTERS OF NORTH AFRICA

If the tide of World War II can be said to have turned at any one point in time, that point occurred in November, 1942. In the foul jungles of Guadalcanal island, as the last Japanese counterattack was hurled back, the United States took a permanent grip on the initiative in the Pacific. In Russia, the ferocious struggle for Stalingrad turned against Hitler as the Red Army encircled 300,000 German troops. And in North Africa, the twin successes of El Alamein and Operation Torch opened wide the gates of opportunity to the Allies.

This opportunity for quick, complete victory in North Africa had to be grasped immediately, however. The first chance came along the coast road west of El Alamein, as Rommel's beaten troops fled before the victorious Eighth Army. If Montgomery could throw an armored flanking column across the road ahead of the remnants of the Panzerarmee, the job begun at such cost at El Alamein would be finished in one stroke.

Montgomery's painstaking battle plan had included a force to pursue the beaten enemy—for Montgomery never doubted that the enemy would be beaten—but the three divisions he named a *corps de chasse* were sucked into the battle and badly mauled. At the very moment of victory, he had to improvise a new *corps de chasse*, one that was neither stocked with extra fuel nor rested and fresh for the chase.

"The essence of an armoured pursuit," wrote a historian of the campaign, "is speed and boldness to the point of foolhardiness." Such a pursuit was, in fact, a perfect example of Rommel's theory of boldness—a driving, headlong rush with much to gain and no real threat to the army if it failed. But this was not Bernard Montgomery's way. He was a

At left two officers of an American reconnaissance patrol in Tunisia study a map as their half-track's crew has a break. Above is the emblem of the U.S. 1st Armored Division, which saw heavy fighting in the Tunisian campaign.

U.S. ARMY

BOTH: IMPERIAL WAR MUSEUM, LONDON

General Montgomery, left, was photographed beside a Grant tank during the pursuit of the Panzer-armee. Rommel's forces were savagely attacked by the RAF; at one point his armored strength stood at less than a dozen tanks.

master of the set-piece engagement, superbly skilled at planning and at preparing an army for battle and in balancing and adjusting forces on the battlefield. It was against his nature to take military risks, to indulge in what he called "mad rush" tactics. Nor, perhaps, was the Rommel legend quite dead. Even in defeat the Desert Fox's reputation inspired a certain caution among his pursuers.

The result was a series of frustrating near-misses. At first the very size of the Eighth Army was a handicap, and the monumental traffic jam that developed as the *corps de chasse* tried to shake free cost some twelve hours. One trap misfired when a British flanking column cut in toward the coast road too soon; another failed when the pursuers stopped for the night while their quarry kept moving. The New Zealanders were held up half a day by a mine field that turned out not only to be a dummy, but a dummy laid by the British themselves during the Gazala Gallop.

Most frustrating of all was the plight of the 1st Armored Division, which made a long dash through the desert toward Matruh—the site of Rommel's dazzling victory the previous June—only to run out of gasoline twice and lose the race. On the evening of November 6, with Rommel's hopes for escape already growing brighter, the heavens opened wide and rain deluged the two armies. On the desert tracks the *corps de chasse* was immediately axle-deep in mud. On the paved coast road the Panzerarmee limped on in the rain—and was finally out of reach.

So one Allied opportunity was lost, but another soon appeared in its place—Tunisia. By quickly seizing and holding this very defensible country, the Torch army could sever Rommel's supply line and leave him hopelessly trapped. Tunisia in fact had once been on the list of Torch's D-day objectives; but with all the other uncertainties, it seemed just too much of a gamble to attempt an amphibious landing under the very nose of the Axis air force in Sicily. Still, the need to strike out fast for Tunisia never left

Jack Chaddock's water color shows an Eighth Army antitank gun unit plodding after Rommel along the coast road in the rain. The Axis forces made liberal use of mines to slow up their pursuers; two signs, one in German and one erected by British engineers, warn drivers not to stray off the road surface.

Eisenhower's thoughts. "This single objective was constantly held before all eyes," he wrote.

There were some 15,000 French troops in Tunisia, poorly armed but strong enough to deny the country to the Axis at least temporarily—if they would fight. Admiral Darlan, however, shrank from ordering the Tunisian garrison to shoot at Germans, even after ordering the shooting at the Allies in Algeria and Morocco to stop. Nor could the French commanders of the garrison bring themselves to put aside notions of military honor and loyalty to Marshal Pétain to act on their own.

U.S. ARMY

General Jürgen von Arnim, veteran of the Russian front, was sent to Tunisia by Hitler to command the newly formed Fifth Panzer Army.

As the hours slipped away and General Clark tried to pin down the squirming Darlan, the Germans scraped up men and guns and hurled them across the Sicilian narrows. French units sat in their weapons pits around the Tunisian airfields and watched impassively as scores of Junkers transport planes spiraled down and landed. Soon a thin line of German troops held the main northern ports of Tunis and Bizerte and the good defensive ground around them and began to trickle southward to "hold the door open" for Rommel.

(It took months to straighten out the troublesome political tangle centered in Algiers. The uproar in the United States and Britain over the so-called Darlan Deal ended only when that unhappy man was assassinated on Christmas Eve, 1942, by a young French patriot. General Giraud then took over, but he proved to be, in President Roosevelt's tart phrase, "a very slender reed" to depend upon. Finally, General de Gaulle brought order out of the confusion. Free French forces were rearmed and eventually played an important role in liberating their homeland from Nazi rule.)

The door of opportunity was still ajar, for the German beachhead was very weak, and the Allies were racing hard for Tunis. More than 550 miles of rugged, mountainous country lay before them. "Get there somehow, and get there quick" was their motto, a war correspondent wrote. "No one quite knew what enemy, if any, was ahead or to the flanks, but morale was up to the limits and there was an infectious air of excitement. . . ." Infantrymen and paratroopers, U.S. Rangers and British commandos, rushed on, never knowing if there would be fuel or ammunition—or food—for the next day.

By mid-November the Allies were well across the Tunisian border but facing stiffening resistance. The Axis poured men into Tunisia at the rate of more than 1,000 a day, a pace the Allies could not match. The Luftwaffe harassed the advancing columns. Nevertheless, a British force pushed to within a dozen miles of Tunis before it was forced back. The race was in its last lap, the outcome was hanging in the balance—and then the rains came.

The soil of northern Tunisia has a peculiar consistency, and overnight it turned into one great soft sea of mud. "Tunisian mire has a flypaper quality all its own," wrote Hollywood producer Darryl Zanuck, a colonel in the Signal Corps. "There are no puddles and you don't slip or splash; you just sink in sort of gentle-like and stay there." General Eisenhower toured the front before a major attack he had scheduled for Christmas Eve. Everywhere he looked the army was bogged down; at one point he watched fascinated as four soldiers tried to get a single motorcycle out of a mud hole, became swamped themselves, and finally left the machine mired deeper than when they began. Bitterly disappointed, he called off the attack. The race for Tunis was over.

UPI

Eisenhower pushed the Torch army hard toward Tunis, reporting that his men were using "every kind of scrawny vehicle that can run."

The stalemate in Tunisia during the winter of 1942–43, like the siege of Tobruk in 1941, was bloody and monotonous and frustrating; only instead of the heat and dust of Tobruk, the troops in Tunisia lived in cold and mud. It was a winter full of those little incidents of war that seemed especially senseless when neither side could gain an advantage. Correspondent Alan Moorehead recorded one such incident, in a village called El Aroussa, in January, 1943.

"The morning broke unusually clear and I wandered into the village," Moorehead wrote. "In the main street half a dozen Tommies were washing in the horse trough, and I fell into conversation with them. They were Londoners, adolescent boys on their first campaign and enjoying a good deal of it. Their backs and chests as they washed were very white, but their faces had gone scarlet through exposure. . . . They were friendly and shy and very determined to do well in the war. . . .

"As I walked back to my camp the Stukas came over. . . . It seemed for a moment that they were going to sail by the village, but at the last moment they altered direction, opened their flaps, and dived. The bombs tumbled out lazily, turning over and over in the morning sunshine. Then with that graceful little jump and a flick, each aircraft turned upward and out of its dive and wheeled away. . . .

"I walked over to the centre of the village, keeping care to stay away from an exploding ammunition lorry. A barn-like building had taken a direct hit, and the coiled barbed wire [stored there] had threshed about wildly in a thousand

ELIOT ELISOFON, *Life* MAGAZINE © TIME INC.

An American infantryman cautiously approaches a Panzer Mark IV smashed by Allied antitank fire in Tunisia. Their long-barreled 75-mm. guns made the Mark IV's dangerous; even more dangerous were the twenty or so Tiger tanks the Germans sent to Tunisia. The Tigers weighed 56 tons, had armor up to four inches thick, and were armed with the notorious tank-killing 88.

murderous tentacles. The blast had carried these fragments across to the water trough, and now my six young friends were curiously huddled up and twisted over one another. It is the stillness of the dead that is so shocking. Even their boots don't seem to lie on the ground as those of a sleeping man would. They don't move at all. They seem to slump into the earth with such unnatural overwhelming tiredness. . . ."

In the desert to the east, meanwhile, the retreat of the Panzerarmee continued. The British pursued doggedly, relentlessly, unable to catch up to Rommel but giving him no rest either. On November 23, for the third time in less than two years, he was back at El Agheila. There the Panzerarmee held for three weeks, gravely wounded but still dangerous, while Montgomery stock-piled supplies for an attack. On December 13, as the British barrage opened, the Desert Fox pulled out.

After another three-week pause at Buerat, some 200 miles to the west, the retreat continued. Tripoli could not be defended, and on January 23, 1943, the Eighth Army marched into the city. Since the days of Wavell and O'Connor, British soldiers had dreamed of taking distant Tripoli, seemingly as unreachable as a desert mirage. Now, wrote a correspondent, they "stood with wonderment and emotion beside the playing fountains"—and then marched on westward. On February 12, the second anniversary of Rommel's arrival in North Africa, the rear guards of the Afrika Korps withdrew across the Libyan border into Tunisia. The Axis dug in at a strong position known as the Mareth Line.

This kind of retreat had gone against all Rommel's instincts. His orders had been to withdraw as slowly as possible, holding off the Eighth Army as long as possible. Rommel favored either withdrawal from North Africa (given Axis supply problems, he believed the campaign was a lost cause) or the classic strategy of an army threatened with entrapment: rapid concentration to defeat the enemy forces in detail before they could combine against him. Every mile Rommel retreated shortened his supply line and lengthened the Eighth Army's, allowing him to retreat a great deal faster than the British could chase him. The Desert Fox had wanted to hurry to Tunisia, combine with General Jürgen von Arnim's Fifth Panzer Army there to rout the still-weak Torch army, and then turn on the Eighth Army while it dangled at the end of its long supply line.

He flew to Germany to raise these matters of new strategy with Hitler. The reaction was, in Rommel's words,

INCIDENT AT KASSERINE PASS

As Rommel's surprise thrust closed in on the American units guarding Kasserine Pass, a reconnaissance unit of the Afrika Korps slipped behind the American lines to seize a small bridge beyond the pass. Its commander, Captain Heinz Schmidt, told of his experience in his book With Rommel in the Desert.

Swiftly I mustered an assault platoon of three officers and 21 men armed with automatic weapons. With as much ammunition as we could carry we crawled through the cover of the undergrowth towards the nearest gully. . . . Our luck held. The gully ran right into the wadi which the bridge crossed. It was not much of a bridge, a little above six feet high and perhaps twelve feet long.

I had two machine guns positioned on either side of the approach to the wadi and the bridge, facing in the direction of the enemy's rear. Darkness dropped suddenly on the valley. And then within minutes, a vehicle approached from the enemy region. As it rolled towards the bridge we tried to hold it up. The truck slowed down, but the men in it recognized us as Germans. One of them fired at us. The truck accelerated and thrashed its way across the bridge before we could recover from our surprise.

That was a lesson. We were wiser when the next vehicle was heard rumbling towards us and loomed up in vague shape in the thickening darkness. The truck came on fast. Both my machine guns let rip at it from either side of the road. The truck swerved off the road and capsized. One of my men leaped up and made prisoners of the men in it—four men, two of them wounded. . . .

A few minutes later six American riflemen were crossing the bridge. They were almost in the middle of it when they were taken with a gasp. Within seconds we heard the sound of another truck approaching. We leaped for cover, and as the truck approached the bridge we turned the machine guns on it. This time our prisoners included three officers. . . .

With the two shot-up trucks I had my men rapidly improvise a road block on the bridge. Several more American trucks ran up to the road block, slowed down, stopped—and we took the men in them without firing a shot. . . .

One of the prisoners was a lieutenant, a breezy character. We chatted away in a strangely cheerful way under that Kasserine bridge about our private affairs. He came from Brooklyn, he said. He lived there with his wife and two children. "A magnificent city," I managed in my broken English. "I should like to see it some day."

"That," he said half-mockingly, "can probably be arranged soon." I got his meaning, and side-stepped: "I think it's going to take us some time to win the war." We both laughed. . . .

Half an hour had passed since the last truck had run into our road block. Now I heard a droning in the distance to the north. The ground began to tremble slightly. Suspicious, I climbed from the wadi to the top of the bank. In the open air the sound of motors purred clearly from where we knew the Americans lay. Enemy tanks, undoubtedly. "If tanks advance on the bridge," I ordered the nearest machine gun, "do not shoot—let them cross." The drone of the engines and the clank of the tracks grew louder. A tank loomed up on the road, appearing colossal against the background of the starry heavens.

The hatch was open, and the commander was standing exposed and looking around. The tank pulled up. "Why this barricade?" his voice rang out. He got no reply. My men had pistols in the ribs of the prisoners below the bridge. The tank commander spoke swiftly to his driver. The tank thrust on, heaving the wrecked trucks to one side.

And then one of our machine guns let rip directly at the tank turret! I had forgotten to ensure that my order reached the gun on the far side of the wadi. Like a rabbit at his hole, the commander dropped down into his turret. The tank sprayed out fire wildly. Thundering, it rolled over the bridge above our heads. The droning went on, and then the rumbling thunder again, the squeak and rattle of tracks.

BUNDESARCHIV, KOBLENZ

Infantrymen of the German 90th Light Division, well muffled against blowing sand, were photographed in 1942.

Another tank passed over the bridge, another and another, one more, then the fifth and last. . . .

The next hour was tense. The American lieutenant from Brooklyn offered me some chewing gum and a cigarette. I seldom smoked, but I felt that a cigarette might do me good. The possibility that I might see Brooklyn, or at least some part of America, before the end of hostilities no longer seemed so remote. . . . I could feel the lieutenant watching me intently. I put on my calmest face. "I'll send out a patrol," I thought, "and if the tanks have definitely pulled off, I must get back. . . ."

"Well, what's happening, bud?" The American lieutenant had moved closer. I shrugged my shoulders indifferently and replied shortly, "Wait!" We dropped into our rather aimless personal conversation again. It was an odd situation. Neither American nor German knew who would be the prisoner next morning. . . .

Then again the droning of tanks, this time from Kasserine. Some distance away the returning tanks opened fire on the bridge. Their cannon shells whammed past and into the bank. Again the shaking of the earth under our feet, the clank and grumble of the tracks, the thunder on the bridge overhead. The tanks went over and on. My machine gunners scrambled back to their positions. The drone of tank engines faded in the distance, like tuneless bagpipes.

The Americans and I looked at each other again. The lieutenant from Brooklyn grinned. "Have some gum, bud," he said. . . .

The men got ready. I turned to the small group of officers, and in my indifferent English told them: "Gentlemen, one of you, together with an ambulance man, may remain with the wounded." I left it to them to decide which of them was to stay behind. They did it swiftly, tossing a coin, heads or tails, eliminating. The final toss lay between a captain and the lieutenant from Brooklyn. Now I was interested too. The coin spun in the darkness again, and dropped to the earth. Heads! The lieutenant had called heads. He was to stay. He was not to be my prisoner, and I was glad of it. . . .

As we left the bridge the lieutenant called out in a whisper: "Good-by, bud—see ya in Berlin!" His mockery was not unpleasant. I called softly: "Auf Wiedersehen—in Brooklyn, when the war is over."

"like a spark in a powder barrel. The Führer flew into a fury. . . . I began to realize that Adolf Hitler simply did not want to see the situation as it was, and that he reacted emotionally against what his intelligence must have told him was right."

Rommel was still determined to seize the initiative if he could. In February, 1943, leaving his infantry in the Mareth Line to hold off Montgomery, he led the Afrika Korps northward for an assault on the Americans in the narrow "waist" of Tunisia. On February 14 the panzers sprang forward to the attack.

Suddenly it was the old glory days all over again—the quick surprise thrust, the reeling enemy, the Desert Fox leading from up front, the waves of consternation spreading through the opposing high command like ripples through a pond after the splash of a stone. Two panzer columns ripped through the thin American line, converged on a mountain gap called Kasserine Pass, brushed aside

Artist Henry Carr painted a 25-pounder, the mainstay of the British artillery, in action in Tunisia in the spring of 1943. The well-handled British artillery was especially effective in the "battles for position" fought in Tunisia.

BOTH: IMPERIAL WAR MUSEUM, LONDON

the force defending it, and poured through the pass into the American rear areas. Desperate counterattacks were methodically chewed up by German tanks and antitank guns.

Collecting every unit they could lay hands on, the Allied commanders labored to plug the gap. Early in the Kasserine battle the green U.S. troops and their inexperienced commanders had been badly knocked about by Rommel's desert veterans; now they began to dig in their heels stubbornly, particularly hard-fighting units of the U.S. 1st Armored Division. "They recovered very quickly after the first shock," Rommel wrote. On February 22, unable to achieve a breakthrough, he pulled back through Kasserine Pass.

Two weeks later, Rommel tried a second attack, this time against the Eighth Army near Mareth. But the old magic was gone. He was exhausted mentally and sick physically, and he handled the attack badly. His armor charged blindly and was cut to pieces by Montgomery's antitank

"Rommel fought every day with something," a British officer wrote of the 1,500-mile Axis retreat after the El Alamein battle. In this picture, Britishers charge an enemy position with fixed bayonets as a casualty receives first aid.

guns; some 50 tanks were lost, while the British lost but half a dozen. On March 9, 1943, his health broken, the Desert Fox left North Africa, never to return.

IMPERIAL WAR MUSEUM, LONDON

The walking wounded: two British soldiers hit in the face during the fighting at the Mareth Line.

By the end of March the Torch army's losses at Kasserine Pass had been made good. Units were consolidated and inept commanders weeded out, and General Alexander arrived from Cairo to command the Allied ground forces. It was now a battle against time, a battle to end the campaign in Tunisia in time to assault Sicily and Italy that summer. If von Arnim could hold out for three or four months, however, no further Allied campaigns would be possible in 1943. This would suit Hitler very well indeed, giving him the chance to concentrate all his forces for one last mighty thrust at Russia.

The terrain facing the Eighth Army in southern Tunisia was on the familiar desert pattern, but the rugged, mountainous north was something else entirely. In desert fighting the armies were spread out and concealed in dust clouds, and the progress of a battle was seldom easy to follow. In northern Tunisia, on the other hand, it was usually possible to see the enemy positions clearly and to plot the course of the battle without difficulty. In the sector manned by the British First Army, for example, there was a long and bitter struggle for a piece of high ground known as Longstop Hill. The climactic British assault on Longstop, made in late April, looked like this to an eyewitness:

"Everything appeared to happen in miniature. The tanks climbing on Jebel Ang looked like toys. The infantry that crept across the uplands toward [the village of] Heidous were tiny dark dots, and when the mortar shells fell among them it was like drops of rain on a muddy puddle. Toy donkeys toiled up the tracks toward the mountain crests, and the Germans, too, were like toys, little animated figures that occasionally got up and ran or bobbed up out of holes in the ground between the shell explosions."

As Longstop was being overrun, another and equally bitter battle was being fought for Hill 609 in the American sector a few miles to the north. This high ground—named for its height in meters on the maps the Allies were using—was blocking the advance of the American 2nd Corps, commanded by Major General Omar Bradley. For four days

The phases of the Tunisian action are shown at right. After Rommel's attack at Kasserine Pass (1) the Allies outflanked the Mareth Line (2) and broke through at Longstop and Hill 609 (3) to threaten Tunis and Bizerte (4).

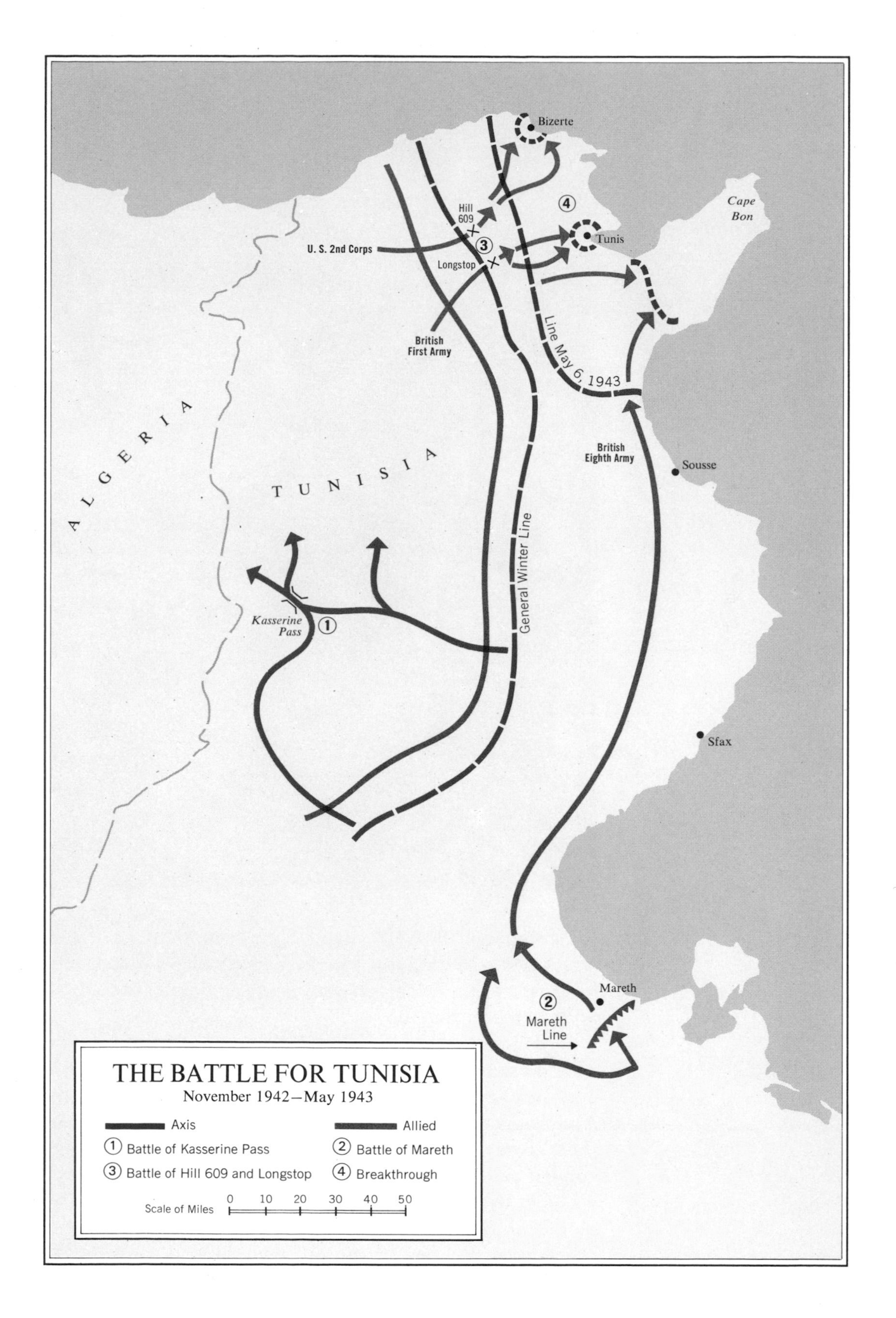
Bizerte
Cape Bon
Hill 609
U. S. 2nd Corps
Longstop
Tunis
British First Army
Line May 6, 1943
A L G E R I A
T U N I S I A
British Eighth Army
Sousse
General Winter Line
Kasserine Pass
Sfax
Mareth
Mareth Line
THE BATTLE FOR TUNISIA
November 1942–May 1943
Axis
Allied
① Battle of Kasserine Pass
② Battle of Mareth
③ Battle of Hill 609 and Longstop
④ Breakthrough
Scale of Miles
0 10 20 30 40 50

Combat artist Fletcher Martin did this view of the savage fighting atop Hill 609, much of it, as depicted here, waged at point-blank range. The American troops at the right, of the 34th Division, make use of the cover of stone walls.

the struggle for Hill 609 raged. Von Arnim's stubborn infantrymen were dug into cracks and crevices on the stony heights, and their mortars and artillery dominated all the approaches to the hill.

"Seldom has an enemy contested a position more bitterly than did the Germans high on Hill 609," wrote General Bradley. They rolled hand grenades down on the Americans clawing for a foothold on the steep slopes, and their strong points were taken only after hand-to-hand combat with pistols, knives, and fists. Each American gain was met by a vicious counterattack. Finally, Bradley ordered Sherman tanks forward to provide fire support. They nosed up to the foot of the hill and chipped away at the

TIME-LIFE COLLECTION, U.S. ARMY

enemy positions with their 75-mm. guns, their armor proof against the bullets and grenades showered down on them.

At last, on May 1, Hill 609 was encircled and the defenders hunted down. The capture was sweet revenge for the U.S. 34th Infantry Division. The 34th had been badly mauled by the Afrika Korps at Kasserine Pass in February, losing both its reputation and its self-respect in the process. Now it regained both, with interest.

Already, Montgomery, in a masterful display of battlefield tactics, had forced the Mareth Line and linked up with the Torch army. The loss of Longstop and Hill 609, combined with heavy pressure from the Eighth Army, drove von Arnim back to his final line of defense overlooking the

duty to report that the Tunisian campaign is over," General Alexander cabled Prime Minister Churchill. "All enemy resistance has ceased. We are the masters of the North African shores."

The crushing defeat in North Africa was the beginning of the end for the Axis partners. Before the year was out, Sicily and Italy were invaded, and massive Russian attacks rolled back the Germans on the eastern front. In June, 1944, the Allies attacked across the English Channel to win a foothold on the Normandy shores; by fall, France was liberated and the battle for Germany had begun.

For some, North Africa was the first step on the road to military fame. Eisenhower became supreme commander of Allied forces in Europe, with Montgomery the head of his ground forces. Alexander commanded the forces in the Mediterranean theater. American generals such as Bradley, blooded in Tunisia, went on to carve important niches for themselves in the European campaign. But for others the desert war was the climax of their military careers. Wavell and Auchinleck, for example, later served in relative obscurity in the Far East; General Ritchie ended up as a corps commander in Europe under Montgomery.

For Erwin Rommel, who put such a unique, personal stamp on the desert war, the future brought only disillusionment and doom. In July, 1944, while commanding the German forces in Normandy, he was gravely wounded in an air attack. A few days later a group of generals, convinced that Hitler was insane and dragging Germany down to destruction in a war already lost, tried to kill the Führer by planting a bomb in his headquarters. Rommel, who had long since come to despise Hitler, knew of the plot to overthrow him but took no part in it. Nor did he know that the conspirators planned to name him head of state to negotiate peace if they succeeded. But Hitler survived, and in the purge that followed, Rommel was implicated.

He was at his home recovering from his wounds when Hitler's police came. They gave him the choice of suicide by poison or a public execution, with its disgrace to his family and his memory. He chose to kill himself. His son, Manfred, saw the body soon afterward. "My father lay on a camp bed in his brown Africa uniform," he said, "a look of contempt on his face." The German people were told that the Desert Fox had died of the wounds suffered in Normandy, and on October 18, 1944, he was given a hero's funeral. Seven months later Hitler too was a suicide, and Germany lay defeated and in ruins.

U.S. ARMY

German prisoners photographed from an observation plane. "This tragedy of three years," correspondent Alan Moorehead wrote of the surrender of the Axis in North Africa, "simply ended with all the actors crowding on to the stage too exhausted to be exultant or defiant or humiliated or resentful."

Veteran tankers lounge against a Crusader in this detail from a 1942 sketch made by Anthony Gross in Egypt.

HORIZON CARAVEL BOOKS

JOSEPH L. GARDNER, *Editor*

Janet Czarnetzki, *Art Director*

Elaine K. Andrews, *Copy Editor*

Sandra L. Russell, *Copy Editor*

Laurie B. Platt, *Picture Researcher*

Gertrudis Feliu, *Chief, European Bureau*

ACKNOWLEDGMENTS

The Editors are particularly grateful for the assistance of Mrs. Mary Jenkins in London. In addition, they would like to thank the following individuals and organizations:

American Field Service, New York—Robert Applewhite

Department of the Air Force, Art and Museum Branch —William Winder

Department of the Army, War Art Collection—George Hobart

Department of the Navy, Combat Art Division—Charles Lawrence

Imperial War Museum, London—W. P. Mayes, J. F. Golding, C. McLaughlin, W. R. Lee

Ministry of Defense, Air Force Library, London—Frank White

National Archives, Enemy Record Division, Washington, D.C.—Dr. Richard Bauer

Maps by Francis & Shaw, Inc.

The quotations from General Rommel's narrative of his North African campaigns and from his letters to his wife are from *The Rommel Papers*, © 1953 by B. H. Liddell Hart (editor), published by Harcourt, Brace & World, Inc. "Incident at Tobruk" (page 34) is from *The Twenty Thousand Thieves* by Eric Lambert, published in 1951 by Newmont Ltd., Melbourne. "Incident at Sidi Rezegh" (pages 52–53) and the description of tank fighting in Operation Crusader (pages 55–58) are taken from Robert Crisp's *Brazen Chariots*, © 1959 by Robert Crisp, published by W. W. Norton & Company, Inc. (first American edition, 1960). "Incident at Kasserine Pass" (pages 136–137) is from *With Rommel in the Desert* by Heinz Werner Schmidt, published in 1951 by G. G. Harrap & Co., Ltd., London. The several accounts by war correspondent Alan Moorehead, including the one on pages 133–135, are from *The March to Tunis*, a 1967 reprinting of his wartime trilogy, © 1943, 1944 by Harper & Row Publishers, Inc. A number of the maps are adapted from those in I. S. O. Playfair's *The Mediterranean and the Middle East* (4 volumes), United Kingdom Military Series, History of the Second World War, Her Majesty's Stationery Office, 1954–66.

FURTHER READING

For those who would like to know more about the desert war and the men who fought it, the following books are recommended:

Agar-Hamilton, J. A. I., and Turner, L. C. F., *Crisis in the Desert: May–July 1942*. Oxford, 1952.

Barnett, Correlli, *The Desert Generals*. Viking, 1961.

Blumenson, Martin, *Kasserine Pass*. Houghton Mifflin, 1967.

Bradley, Omar N., *A Soldier's Story*. Holt, 1951.

Carver, Michael, *Tobruk*. Batsford, 1964.

Churchill, Winston S., *The Second World War*, Vols. 2–4. Houghton Mifflin, 1949–50.

Clark, Mark W., *Calculated Risk*. Harper, 1950.

Connell, John, *Wavell: Scholar and Soldier*. Harcourt, 1964.

Cowles, Virginia, *The Phantom Major*. Harper, 1958.

Crisp, Robert, *Brazen Chariots*. Norton, 1960.

Eisenhower, Dwight D., *Crusade in Europe*. Doubleday, 1949.

Howe, George F., *Northwest Africa: Seizing the Initiative in the West* (United States Army in World War II). Department of the Army, 1957.

Kippenberger, Howard, *Infantry Brigadier*. Oxford, 1949.

Liddell Hart, B. H., ed., *The Rommel Papers*. Harcourt, 1953.

———*The Tanks*. Cassell, 1959.

Lucas Phillips, C. E., *Alamein*. Little, Brown, 1962.

Macintyre, Donald, *The Battle for the Mediterranean*. Norton, 1965.

Majdalany, Fred, *The Battle of El Alamein*. Lippincott, 1965.

Montgomery, Bernard, *Memoirs*. World, 1958.

Moorehead, Alan, *The March to Tunis: the North African War, 1940–1943*. Harper, 1967 (*African Trilogy*, Hamish Hamilton, 1944, 1966).

Morison, Samuel Eliot, *Operations in North African Waters* (History of U.S. Naval Operations in World War II, Vol. 2). Little, Brown, 1957.

Murphy, Robert, *Diplomat Among Warriors*. Doubleday, 1964.

Playfair, I. S. O., *The Mediterranean and the Middle East* (United Kingdom Military Series), 4 vols. Her Majesty's Stationery Office, 1954–66.

Schmidt, Heinz, *With Rommel in the Desert*. Harrap, 1951.

Tomkins, Peter, *The Murder of Admiral Darlan*. Simon & Schuster, 1965.

Young, Desmond, *Rommel: The Desert Fox*. Harper, 1950.

INDEX

Boldface indicates pages on which maps or illustrations appear

The crew of a Grant brews up for a hot meal at day's

IMPERIAL WAR MUSEUM, LONDON

end, a brief, quiet, treasured time for both armies.